Guide to
Study Skills
and Strategies

Globe
Fearon

Upper Saddle River, New Jersey
www.globefearon.com

Project Reviewers

Phyllis Scrivano Klemstein, M. Ed.
Special Educator
O. W. Holmes High School
San Antonio, Texas

Elizabeth Rzemieniewski, M. Ed.
Special Education Coordinator
Olney High School
Philadelphia, Pennsylvania

Susan Simone-Vidal
Special Educator
Summit Middle School
Summit, New Jersey

Project Editor: Brian Hawkes
Editorial Assistants: Jennifer Keezer, Jenna Thorsland
Interior Design: Tricia Battipede
Production Editor: Alan Dalgleish
Electronic Page Production: José López, Jeffrey Engel
Manufacturing Supervisor: Mark Cirillo
Cover Design: Tricia Battipede
Illustrator: Edward Briant, Andre V. Malok

Printed in the United States of America.
   4 5 6 7 8 9 10   04 03 02 01

ISBN 0-130-23231-9

Contents

part **two**
CONTENT-AREA STUDY SKILLS 118

To The Student

WHAT ARE STUDY SKILLS AND STRATEGIES?

Have you ever studied hard for a test and not done as well as you thought you should have? You may have thought 'Why should I study? I studied hard and still did not do well.'

You may have spent enough time studying. However, you may not have made the most out of your study time. If you did not have the right tools to help you study, you probably did not make the most out of your study time.

Think of study skills and strategies as tools. For example, a mechanic needs to know how to use his tools before he or she can work on a car. If the mechanic does not know how to use his or her tools, he or she will have a hard time fixing anything!

Study skills and strategies are the tools you need to become better at studying. Once you have learned how to use these tools, you will be able to make the most out of your study time.

WHY ARE STUDY SKILLS IMPORTANT?

Study skills and strategies are important because they give you a plan for studying. Once you have learned the study skills and strategies in this book studying will be easier—and probably more fun. You will learn how to get the most out of your study time. You will learn skills and strategies that will work for you.

In addition to helping you study, the skills and strategies will be useful to you outside of school. Whether it is in the workplace or at home, you will find that the skills and strategies will help you in your life.

HOW TO GET THE MOST OUT OF THIS BOOK

Using the Part Introductions   You can use the part introduction to preview what you will be learning in each part of this book. You will also be able to use the "Brainstorm!" questions to discuss study issues with your peers. Make sure you share your ideas with your classmates.

Using the Chapter Introductions   Each Chapter Introduction starts off with a short story. Pay attention to the problems these characters face. They may be problems you have faced.

Using the Lessons   Each lesson in Part 1 follows the same three-step format:

STEP 1: A topic is introduced to you.

STEP 1: The topic is modeled for you.

STEP 3: You get a chance to try the topic on your own.

Using the In Real Life/In the Workplace   "In Real Life"/"In the Workplace" appears in each chapter. The skill or strategy you learned about in the chapter is put into a real life or workplace setting. You can see how the skills and strategies you learned will help you outside of the classroom.

Using the Chapter Reviews   The Chapter Review is in a checklist format. When you review these pages, check off what you have learned. If you are unclear about any of the items on the list, go back to the lesson and review it again.

Using the Chapter Practices   The Chapter Practice gives you a chance to practice what you have learned. You will be asked to recall the skills and strategies you learned in the chapter.

Using the Learning Styles Checklist
The Learning Styles Checklist will help you learn more about the way you learn. The checklist gives you ideas for how to make the most out of your unique learning style.

Using the Part Wrap-Ups   In the Part Wrap-Ups, you will create an "action plan." Once you fill in your "action plan," you can use it as a reference tool. The next time you sit down to study, you can look back and see if you are using your study skills and strategies.

HOW THIS BOOK WILL MAKE YOU A BETTER LEARNER

This book will make you a better learner in two ways. First, it will give you the skills and strategies you need to study effectively. Second, you will learn more about your learning style. Your teachers and parents can help you, but only you know what works best for you.

part**one**

GENERAL STUDY SKILLS

As a student, you are used to studying for all of your classes. Of course, you need to spend time studying. Spending time studying is important, but it is not the only thing you need to do. The topics taught in this unit will help you make the most out of your study time.

Here is what you will learn in Part I:

CHAPTER 1
Setting Goals for Yourself

CHAPTER 2
Organizing Yourself

CHAPTER 3
Using Your Resources

CHAPTER 4
Understanding What You Read

CHAPTER 5
Note Taking In Class

CHAPTER 6
Note Taking From Textbooks

CHAPTER 7
Memory Strategies

CHAPTER 8
Test Taking

Brainstorm!

One of the lessons in Part I talks about the things you need to help you study. These things can include anything from a pencil to a well-lit study space. In small groups, make a list of materials you need to study. Share your list with the class.

Chapter ONE

Setting Goals for Yourself

BASKETBALL DREAMS

Both Juan and Tony liked basketball. They were pretty good players. Both boys thought it would be cool to be on the school basketball team next year.

At home, Juan taped this note on his mirror: "I'm going to play for the Bobcats next year!" To get better, Juan joined a summer basketball league. He shot baskets with his brother. He read books about basketball. On weekends he played at the schoolyard.

Tony wanted to play for the Bobcats too. He thought Juan's note was silly. Tony did not bother joining the summer league. Sometimes he played down at the schoolyard. He saw that Juan was getting better.

In November, both boys went out for the team. Juan made it, but Tony did not. "Hey, what happened?" asked Tony. "I used to be better than you!"

What happened? That is simple. Juan set a goal for himself. Then he worked to make it happen. Tony did not set a clear goal, so there was nothing for him to work toward. In this chapter, you will learn about the importance of setting—and reaching—goals.

What Do You Think?

▶ Why is it important to set clear goals for yourself?

▶ Why is it hard to stick with a goal? Why is it so easy to give up?

LESSON 1
Creating Goals for Yourself

Imagine playing basketball without any baskets. You would not have anything to shoot for. In life, goals are like baskets. They give you something to shoot for. Goals help you decide what you want and help you get it!

Take a Look

DAILY GOALS

In school, some goals are daily goals. They are things you must do in the next day or two. Get in the habit of writing daily goals every day. You will feel good as you reach each goal and check it off.

Look at the daily goals Wendy set for herself: ➤

> **Daily Goals**
> 1. Read pages 220-234 in social science text.
> 2. Work on problems 6-14 on page 176 in math.

SHORT-TERM GOALS

Some goals take a week, a month, or a few months to reach. These are short-term goals. Short-term goals focus on projects and tasks that are coming up soon.

Look at the short-term goals Brian set for himself: ➤

> **Short-Term Goals**
> 1. Write essay for social science class.
> 2. Practice for piano recital.

LONG-TERM GOALS

So far you've looked at daily goals and short-term goals. Other goals take a lot longer. They are long-term goals. They may take a year or more to reach.

Having long-term goals is important. You cannot reach these goals overnight. You must know your long-term goals so you can start to work toward them.

Remember, many long-term goals can be divided into short-term goals and daily goals. When you set a long-term goal, think of what you will need to do to achieve your goal. Look at the long-term goals Tricia set for herself: ►

Long-Term Goals
1. Graduate high school.
2. Own a house.

Try It Out

On the following lines, a long-term goal is given. A short-term goal that supports the long-term goal is also given. Fill in another short-term goal and two daily goals that support the long-term goal of buying a car.

Long-term goal: _Buy a car._____

Short-term goal: _____

Short-term goal: _Get a part-time job._____

Daily goal: _____

Daily goal: _____

On Your Own

On the lines below, create a long-term goal for yourself. Then write two short-term goals and two daily goals that will help you achieve your long-term goal.

Long-term goal: _____

Short-term goal: _____

Short-term goal: _____

Daily goal: _____

Daily goal: _____

LESSON 2
Achieving Your Goals

Goals are like the baskets in a gym. When you play basketball, though, it is not enough to have baskets. You also need to get the ball through them! In the same way, setting goals is not enough. You also have to reach, or achieve, your goals.

Take a Look

REACHING DAILY GOALS

Make your daily goals specific. For a daily goal, note when and where you plan to reach it. Give yourself a reason for reaching it.

Read Kendra's daily goals. She lists where and when she will reach each goal. She also gives a simple reason for each goal.

1. Study Chapters 3 and 4 of math tonight for at least 90 minutes after dinner. There will be a quiz in class on this!

2. Go to Mr. Gomez's extra help class in Room 314 at 3:00 P.M. Students with less than an 80 average have to go.

Follow up on your daily goals each day. Check off the goals you have reached. They are something to feel good about!

REACHING SHORT-TERM AND LONG-TERM GOALS

With short-term and long-term goals, you also need to list where and when you will reach each goal. You should also give a reason for each goal. Break your short-term and long-term goals into the daily goals needed to reach them. This will keep you on the right track.

Read John's long-term goal on the top of the next page. Then look at the short-term and daily goals he created to help him reach his long-term goal.

> **Long-term goal:** Go to college. Four years from now I would like to be in college. I want to be a doctor. I need to go to college to become a doctor.
>
> **Short-term goal:** Look into colleges. I need to find a college that will help me become a doctor.
>
> **Daily goal:** Talk to my guidance counselor after school. She will help me find the right college.

Time is very important in reaching short-term and long-term goals. By breaking your long-term goals into short-term and daily goals, you will be able to reach your long term goals.

Try It Out

On the following lines, Pablo has set a long-term goal. Fill in a short-term goal and a daily goal that support the long-term goal.

Long-term goal: <u>When I graduate from high school, I would like</u>

<u>to become a police officer.</u>

Short-term goal: _____

Daily goal: _____

On Your Own

Now think of your own long-term goal. Then write a short-term goal and a daily goal that will help you reach your long-term goal. Remember to include where and when you will reach these goals and your reasons for these goals.

Long-term goal: _____

Short-term goal: _____

Daily goal: _____

Denzel wants to work at Camp Evergreen this summer. It is a day camp for children. The application asks about his goals for working. Setting and reaching goals will help you in the workplace.

CAMP EVERGREEN   **JOB APPLICATION**

1. Name <u>Taylor   Denzel   F</u>
       (last)   (first)   (middle)

2. Address <u>1   Elm Street</u>
           (no)   (street)

   <u>Elm   New York   55555</u>
    (city)   (state)   (zip code)

3. Telephone <u>555-1234</u> Birth date <u>11/16/1984</u>

4. Job you are applying for: <u>camp counselor</u>.

5. Why do you want to work at this summer job?

   <u>Day camp was great for me when I was younger. Now I would like</u>

   <u>to help other kids have a good summer.</u>

6. What are your goals?

   <u>My long-term goal is to be a gym teacher. My short-term goal is</u>

   <u>to save money for college. Being a camp counselor will help me</u>

   <u>reach these goals.</u>

YOUR TURN

Your teacher will provide you with a blank job application. Choose a job you are interested in and fill out your own job application.

Chapter One

REVIEW

You have learned a lot already! Look at the checklist and check off what you have learned.

When I set daily goals for myself, I:

☐ list the things I want to get done in the next day or so. (Lesson 1)

☐ note where and when I plan to reach each goal. (Lesson 2)

☐ give a reason why I want to reach the goal. (Lesson 2)

☐ check off each goal I reach. (Lesson 2)

When I set short-term goals for myself, I:

☐ list things I should do over the next few weeks or months. (Lesson 1)

☐ set a due date or deadline for each goal. (Lesson 2)

☐ give a reason why the goal is important. (Lesson 2)

When I set long-term goals for myself, I:

☐ list things I hope to achieve in years to come. (Lesson 1)

☐ find out as much as I can about the goal. (Lesson 2)

☐ break my long-term goals into short-term and daily goals. (Lesson 2)

CHAPTER ONE PRACTICE

Answer the following items about what you have learned in this chapter.

1. Decide whether each goal is a daily goal, a short-term goal, or a long-term goal. Write *daily*, *short-term*, or *long-term* on the line next to each goal.

   a. Read pages 113-118 in social studies text for a quiz tomorrow. _____

   b. Paint the scenery for the class play next month.

   _____

   c. Go to community college to study landscaping.

   _____

   d. See Mr. Falco about making up the English test I missed. _____

   e. Write a term paper about ancient Rome. _____

   f. Get married and raise a family. _____

   g. Join the Navy to become an electrician. _____

   h. Get all *B*s on my report card this term. _____

   i. Study Spanish with Alberto tonight. _____

2. Which type of goal should be done in the next few weeks or months? Circle the correct answer.

   a. a daily goal

   b. a short-term goal

   c. a long-term goal

3. List three daily goals for yourself.

   a. _____

   b. _____

   c. _____

4. When you write a daily or short-term goal, you should write the _____ each goal is important. You should also set a _____ for finishing. These things will help you reach your goals.

5. Rewrite these daily and short-term goals. Add details that will help the person reach the goal.

   a. Make a Halloween costume for the party.

   _____

   _____

   b. Talk to Mr. Diaz about my book report.

   _____

   _____

   c. Memorize my lines for the play.

   _____

   _____

Talk It Over

With a group of classmates, talk about what you have learned. Answer these questions in your discussion:

▶ How can setting goals help you in school and in life?

▶ What can you do to make sure you achieve your goals?

chapter one

LEARNING STYLES CHECK-IN

Everyone learns in different ways. What type of learner are you? Check off the ways you learn best. Then use the suggestions to help you set or reach your goals.

Word-smart learner
- Find a story or poem about the importance of goals. Read it aloud to the class.

Sound-smart learner
- Tape-record your short-term and long-term goals. Play the tape every so often.

People-smart learner
- Set goals with a friend. Talk with others about how they reach goals.

Self-smart learner
- Write a journal entry that lists your goals and tells why they are important.

Picture-smart learner
- Draw pictures that show a goal or goals. Show yourself reaching a long-term goal.

Action-smart learner
- Make a goal holder. Use wood, cardboard, or other materials to make an object to display your written goals.

Number-smart learner
- Make a chart that shows the steps toward reaching one of your goals. For each step, tell what you must do or solve.

Chapter
TWO

Organizing Yourself

SONDRA'S TEST

On Sunday morning, Sondra remembered that she had left her notebook at school. So she went to Denise's to copy her notes. They went downtown to find a copy machine. They also did some shopping. It was 1:00 P.M. when Sondra got home.

Sondra sat down in the living room to study. Her brother Ben was watching a movie. Before long, Sondra got interested in the movie.

After the movie, Sondra went to the kitchen. She liked to study at the kitchen table. Dad was cooking and listening to music. Sondra decided to help Dad cook. It was time for a break.

After dinner, Sondra went to her room to study. There was too much stuff on her desk, so she lay on her bed. Because Sondra was not sure what the test would cover, she called Chantal. They talked for an hour. After Chantal hung up, Sondra dozed off.

"Bedtime, Sondra," her mother called. "Ready for your test?"

"I think so," said Sondra. "I've been studying all day."

What happened? Sondra spent all day trying to study. But she did not really study very much. For one thing, Sondra did not have the materials she needed. She did not have a study space either. Sondra also wasted a lot of her study time. In this chapter, you will learn about the importance of organizing yourself to study well.

What Do You Think?

▶ Why is it important to study in an organized way?

▶ What are some ways to organize yourself to study?

LESSON 1
Finding Your Study Space

To do their jobs well, mechanics need the right space. Right now, studying is your job. To do it well, you need the right study space and the right study tools.

Take a Look

There are many places to study. The library is one good place. It is quiet, and there are books to use. Your school might have a study hall for students. Most students study at home though. A home study space is the most handy.

Here are three good study spaces:

1. Glen keeps all his study material in his backpack. He goes to the library to study.
2. Vera goes to her aunt's house each day after school. There she works at a table in the spare room.
3. Toshio has a small desk in the room he shares with his brother. Each night, he studies there after dinner.

What can you do to make a good study space? Here are some do's and don'ts to think about:

 Do

- Have a bright lamp that lights up your whole desk or table.
- Keep your study area neat.
- Sit in a comfortable, straight-backed chair.

 Don't

- Let a loud radio, TV, or music bother you.
- Study in an area where others interrupt you.
- Keep magazines, games, and toys on your desk.

Try It Out

Write three problems with the study space in this drawing.

1. _____

2. _____

3. _____

You have to find a study space that is right for you. Usually, that means a quiet, pleasant place. Most people study best sitting on a chair with a book propped up on a desk.

On the other hand, you have to be comfortable. Maybe soft music helps you study. If so, play it. Maybe a scent like lemon makes you relax. Some people like to move a bit when studying. They rock their chairs, tap their feet, or walk around. Be creative! Make the study space that is right for you.

On Your Own

On the following lines, describe the place where you study or draw it on a separate sheet of paper. Then, list what you can do to make it a better study space.

_____

_____

LESSON 2
Organizing Your Time

Key Terms

study calendar weekly calendar that lists the things you have to do
study clock an hour by hour list of what you need to study

Sports, clubs, after-school jobs—students live busy lives. No wonder they can lose track of time. Somehow, students have to find time to study too. On busy days, that can be hard to do.

Take a Look

STUDY CALENDARS

A **study calendar** is a good way to organize your time. You can make one each week. On the calendar, list everything you have to do that week. That means school activities, jobs, parties, whatever! Once you list everything, look for the openings. Those are times you have to study. Keep your calendar handy. Look at it every day.

Here is Colin's weekly calendar. Look carefully at each day. What afternoons and evenings does Colin have to study?

MONDAY	TUESDAY	WEDNESDAY	THURSDAY	FRIDAY
soccer practice 3:00–5:30	Study time 5:00–6:00	soccer practice 3:00–5:30	soccer practice 3:00–5:30	
Dinner 6:00–7:00	Dinner 6:00–7:00	Dinner 6:00–7:00	Dinner 6:00–7:00	Dinner 6:00–7:00
Study time 7:00–8:00	Orchestra 7:30–10:00	study time 7:00–10:00	Climbing Club 8:00–10:00	

STUDY CLOCKS

A study calendar tells when you have time to study. You also have to decide what to study—and for how long. For that, you need a **study clock**.

A study clock is an hour-by-hour list. It shows exactly what you will study and when. For example, Colin wrote study time from 7–10 P.M. on Wednesday night. His study clock for this time might look like this:

Wednesday Evening Study Clock	
7:00–7:30	Read Social Studies, pp. 123–134 and do worksheet.
7:30–8:30	Rewrite English essay, make editing suggestions.
8:30–9:00	Dinner and TV break.
9:00–10:00	Study Chapter 11 for Math quiz.

 When you make a study clock, check your daily goals. See page 10.

Try It Out

Here are Colin's partly filled-in study calendar and study clock. Colin also needs to visit his aunt, buy his sister a birthday gift, and read a novel. Help him fill in the rest. Which afternoons and evenings are free for Colin? Mark them with a star.

MONDAY	TUESDAY	WEDNESDAY	THURSDAY	FRIDAY
soccer practice 4:00–5:30 Dinner 6:00–7:00	Dinner 6:00–7:00 study time 7:00–10:00	soccer practice 4:00–5:30 Dinner 6:00–7:00	Dinner 6:00–7:00 study time 7:00–10:00	soccer practice 4:00–5:30 Dinner 6:00–7:00

Tuesday Evening Study Clock	
7:00–7:30	Read novel for English class.
7:30–8:30	
8:30–10:00	

On Your Own

Create your own study calendar. What times are open for study in the next two days? List them on a separate sheet of paper. Make a study clock for each time slot. Show what you will study and for how long.

LESSON 3
Doing Homework

Key Term

assignment pad notebook where you list all of your homework assignments

Have you ever had trouble cooking something? If you did not have everything you needed, the dish would not turn out well. Doing homework is similar. You need to have everything ready at your study space. Your mind needs to be ready too.

Take a Look

HOMEWORK MATERIALS

Three homework materials are most important:

- First, you need your **assignment pad**. Your assignment pad tells you exactly what you need to do.

- You also need your textbooks. You may have to read the text for homework. You may have to answer questions in the text.

- Finally, you need your notebook. Your notebook has your notes from class.

A "HOMEWORK-FRIENDLY" ATTITUDE

Sasha empties her backpack to find the things she needs to do her math and English homework. She pulls out her algebra textbook and math notebook. She finds her grammar workbook and English notebook. Finally, she finds her assignment pad under everything else.

You may need other homework materials. You will need pens and pencils. You will need paper. Rulers, staplers, and a calculator are important too. Keep them at your study space. Then you will not waste time looking for them.

Having all your homework materials is not enough. You must get your mind ready too. Do you have a bad attitude toward homework? Do you think it is a waste of time? Do you put it off?

Try to be "homework friendly." Remember, homework helps you learn. It helps you prepare for tests. Doing homework helps you succeed. Every student has to do it.

Here are some ways to get homework friendly:

- Pay attention in class. Then homework makes more sense.
- Ask a teacher for help if you do not understand homework.
- Do not fight against your homework. Just do it!

Try It Out

Write the homework materials you see at this study space.

_____   _____

_____   _____

_____   _____

On Your Own

On the following lines, tell why it is important to make sure you have all your study materials before you sit down to study.

_____

_____

LESSON 4
Making the Most of Your Study Time

Some people like ice cream more than spinach. Still, they know it is important to eat a balanced meal. To be healthy, they eat vegetables first. Then they have dessert. Similarly, most students like some subjects more than others. Often they study their favorite subjects first. Less favorite subjects get less—or no—time.

Take a Look

Always balance your study time. That means spending more time on subjects that give you trouble. That is the only way to do better in them. Hard as it sounds, do the work you like least first!

Cicely's favorite subject is English. On Tuesday night, she decided to rewrite her English essay for the third time. True, she did have a math test the next day. Math was her least favorite subject. Still, Cicely wanted her essay to be perfect. She worked on it for half an hour. Then she had to call Mrs. Butler about baby-sitting. She went back to work on the essay. Then she had to call her father. At 10:00 P.M., Cicely was finally happy with the rewrite. She opened the math book to study. She was just too tired to read!

Why should Cicely have worked on math before she worked on English?

_____

_____

_____

_____

It is easy to waste time when studying. Look at the list of some do's and don'ts on the top of the next page. Use this list to help you make the most of your study time.

Do

- Get phone calls and chores out of the way before you begin.
- Use a study calendar and a study clock to help you plan your study time.
- Work on your least favorite subjects first.

 Don't

- Try to study when you are hungry, thirsty, or very tired.
- Get nervous if you fall behind in a subject. Just change your study schedule. Make more time for the subject.
- Waste time trying to make one project or paper "perfect."
- Work on your favorite subjects first.

Try It Out

Write your two favorite subjects on the following lines. Note the last grade you got in each. Then write your two least favorite subjects. Note your grades for them too. Finally, draw a star next to the subjects that you should spend the most time studying.

Favorite subjects:

_____

_____

Least favorite subjects:

_____

_____

On Your Own

On the following lines, describe some things you can do to use your study time better.

_____

_____

Study calendars and clocks are schedules. They help you organize your time.

Bus and train schedules also help you keep track of time. These schedules show how long a trip takes. That lets you plan how much time you will need.

The schedule below shows the morning stops on one bus line. The bus stops are at the top of the schedule. The times when a bus reaches a stop are listed below the stop.

Weekday Bus Service--Route 63, Holmdale to Emery					
State & Washington	Curry & Harlan	Route 11 Alton	Big Six Mall	Pine Plaza	City Hall
6:10	6:28	6:35	6:40	6:48	7:05
----	----	----	7:00	7:08	7:25
6:50	7:08	7:15	7:20	7:28	7:45
----	----	----	7:40	7:48	8:05
7:30	7:48	7:55	8:00	8:08	8:25
----	----	----	8:20	8:28	8:45

In order to figure out the time it will take to get from one place to another, all you have to do is subtract the time you leave one place from the time you arrive in another.

For example, if you are taking the 6:10 bus from State and Washington to the Big Six Mall, it would take 30 minutes. 6:40−6:10 = 30 minutes.

YOUR TURN

Use the bus schedule to answer these questions.

1. How long is the bus ride from State and Washington streets to Pine Plaza? _____

2. Ramon missed the 7:20 bus at the Big Six Mall. How long will he have to wait for the next bus? _____

Chapter Two

REVIEW

You have learned a lot already! Look at the checklist and check off what you have learned. You can add some of your own ideas on the lines following the checklist.

When I study, I:

☐ have a comfortable, quiet study space. (Lesson 1)

☐ try to work in the same place every day. (Lesson 1)

☐ use a study calendar to plan when I will study. (Lesson 2)

☐ make a study clock to decide what and how long I will study. (Lesson 2)

☐ use my daily goals to plan my study time. (Lesson 2)

☐ arrange all the homework materials I will need before studying. (Lesson 3)

☐ make sure I have an assignment pad, textbooks, and notebooks nearby when I do my homework. (Lesson 3)

☐ have a "homework-friendly" attitude. (Lesson 3)

☐ decide which subjects I need to study most. (Lesson 4)

☐ study my least favorite subjects first. (Lesson 4)

☐ _____

☐ _____

☐ _____

☐ _____

Answer the following items about what you have learned in this chapter.

1. Place a check next to places that are *not* good study spaces. Then work with a partner to discuss your answers.

    _____ **a.** the local library

    _____ **b.** a local teen hangout or diner

    _____ **c.** a friend or relative's house

    _____ **d.** your bedroom at home

    _____ **e.** the schoolyard after school

    _____ **f.** the kitchen table while relatives are preparing a meal

    _____ **g.** an after-school study hall

2. List two problems with Jake's study space.

    a. _____

    b. _____

3. Why is it a good idea to make a study calendar each week?

_____

_____

4. Suppose you plan to study from 7:00 to 10:00 P.M. tonight. Make a study clock that shows what you will do during this time. Make sure you list the subjects you need to study. Also list the time you plan on spending on each subject.

_____

_____

_____

5. What three homework materials are most important? Write the three things you should have with you when doing homework.

a. _____

b. _____

c. _____

6. Check two ways to become "homework friendly."

☐ Think of homework as a waste of time.

☐ Ask for help if you have trouble with homework.

☐ Pay more attention in class.

☐ Put off your homework.

Talk It Over

With a group of classmates, talk about what you have learned.

Answer these questions:

▶ How can a study calendar help you organize your time?

▶ Why is it a good idea to use a study clock?

LEARNING STYLES CHECK-IN

Check off the ways you learn best. Then use the suggestions to help get yourself organized to study.

Word-smart learner

- Take pride in the answers you write for homework. Find the words that say exactly what you want them to.

Sound-smart learner

- Find some peaceful music to play softly in the background while you study. Choose something that puts you in the mood to think!

People-smart learner

- Consider studying with a friend. A study partner can make it easier to study and do homework.

Self-smart learner

- Decide how you will reward yourself after each hour of study. A reward can be a snack, a short chat on the telephone, a chapter of a mystery novel—whatever!

Picture-smart learner

- Sketch what your ideal study space will look like. Then work to make it happen.

- When you study, pay special attention to the pictures in the text. They will help you learn.

Action-smart learner

- Activity might help you study. When it is time for a study break, lift weights, take a short jog, or shoot some baskets. As you unwind, think about what you have been studying.

Number-smart learner

- Make a bar graph that shows how much time you spend each week studying each subject.

Chapter
THREE

Using Your Resources

DALE'S DILEMMA

Dale had to write about the space shuttle. He had a problem though. He could not find information. First, Dale looked up *space shuttle* in the dictionary. All he found was its meaning.

"I should go to the library," Dale said. However, Dale did not know how to use the library computer. So he walked around looking for books. He could not find any on the shuttle. So Dale left without any books.

"Maybe you can use the Internet," Dale's mother said. So Dale signed on. He typed in *space* and got 20 million sources. He started to go through them. After two hours, he was still looking for something about the shuttle.

"There just is nothing!" Dale said. "I need more resources!"

What happened? Actually, Dale had enough resources. He had problems using them though. For example, he should have looked up *space shuttle* in an encyclopedia. He should have learned how to use the library computer. Dale also needs practice with the Internet. When he uses these resources well, he will be a better student.

What Do You Think?

▶ What are some resources you use when studying?

▶ Why is it important to know how to use resources well?

LESSON 1
What Are Study Resources?

Key Term
study resources sources that help you get information

Every country has resources. Land, water, and workers are resources. A country uses resources. Resources make life better.

All students have **study resources**. Study resources can make you a better student.

Take a Look

Jason has many study resources. First, he uses his father's dictionary when doing homework. For other reference books, he goes to the local library. It is a short walk from his house. The library has the Internet too. He has to sign up ahead of time to use it.

REFERENCE BOOKS

The dictionary, thesaurus, and encyclopedia are study resources. They are reference books. Try to have them in your study space.

Dictionary.   A dictionary lists all English words. It tells how to spell and say each word. It gives the meaning of the word too.

Thesaurus.   A thesaurus is also a word book. It lists synonyms for common words. Synonyms are words with similar meanings, like *hot* and *sizzling*. Use a thesaurus to find the exact word to use.

Encyclopedia.   An encyclopedia is a book of information. It gives information on most topics. The information can fill a whole set of books.

OTHER STUDY RESOURCES

Sometimes, you need the most up-to-date facts. Sometimes, you need a map. Here are the resources to use:

Atlas.   An atlas is a book of maps. Use it if you have a question about a place.

Almanac. An almanac is a book of useful facts. It comes out every year. It has up-to-date information.

Periodicals. Newspapers and magazines are periodicals. Use them to find recent information.

Try It Out

Which study resource would be the best place to look first to answer each question? Write *dictionary, thesaurus, encyclopedia, atlas, almanac,* or *periodicals.*

1. When did John Glenn become the first American in space?

     _____

2. What is the meaning of *lunar module*? _____

3. How far from Miami, Florida is the shuttle-launching site

     at Cape Canaveral? _____

4. What words have about the same meaning as *orbit*?

     _____

5. Who are the astronauts in next week's shuttle flight?

     _____

6. How many flights has the space shuttle *Atlantis* made over the

     last three years? _____

On Your Own

Choose a topic that interests you. Tell how you might use three different study resources to find out about your topic.

_____

_____

_____

_____

LESSON 2

When to Use the Dictionary, Thesaurus, and Encyclopedia

The dictionary, encyclopedia, and thesaurus are important. These resources are books or on CD-ROMs. Using them will help you do well in school.

Take a Look

USING A DICTIONARY

Does *satellite* have one or two *l*'s? What does *cosmonaut* mean? How do you pronounce *rendezvous*? A dictionary answers most questions about a word.

Read this dictionary entry. Notice what it tells you. First it tells the spelling. This is followed by the pronunciation and part of speech. Then the meaning is given. Finally, the word is used in a sentence.

> **orbit**   (OHR bit) *n.* the path of a celestial body or satellite as it revolves around another body. *The moon's* orbit *around the earth takes 28 days.*

USING A THESAURUS

English has many, many words. Almost every word has synonyms. Synonyms are words with similar meanings. A thesaurus lists all the synonyms of a word. If you look up *spacecraft* in a thesaurus, you might find an entry like this:

> **spacecraft:**   spaceship, shuttle, shuttle engine, rocket, booster, thruster, retrorocket.

Use the thesaurus carefully. Each synonym has a slightly different meaning. Choose the word that means just what you want to say.

USING AN ENCYCLOPEDIA

You can use an encyclopedia to find facts. An encyclopedia has information on most topics. Often the information fills a whole set of books. The topics in an encyclopedia are in alphabetical order. Look up the topic you want to learn about.

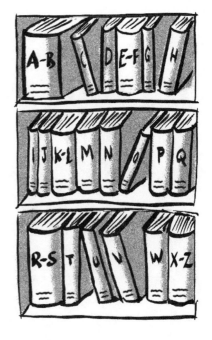

Try It Out

Dale is writing about the space shuttle. As he writes, a few problems come up. Write which reference source Dale should use to solve each problem: *dictionary*, *thesaurus*, or *encyclopedia*.

1. Dale notices that he is using the word *astronauts* in almost every sentence of his paper.

   _____

2. Dales uses the word *trajectory*. He is confused about what it means though.

   _____

3. To describe the shuttle's takeoff, Dale needs facts about how fast the shuttle moves to escape Earth's gravity.

   _____

On Your Own

1. Use a dictionary to find the meaning of these words.

   a. trajectory: _____

   b. aerospace: _____

2. Use a thesaurus to find two synonyms for each of these words.

   a. astronaut: _____   _____

   b. interplanetary: _____   _____

3. Use an encyclopedia to find two facts about the space shuttle.

   a. _____

   b. _____

LESSON 3
Getting the Most Out of Your Library

Key Term

call number number that indicates where you can find a book in the library

The library is a great study resource. You can learn just about anything there. Of course, you need to know how to use the library!

Most libraries have computer catalogs. This catalog lists all the items in the library. Using a computer catalog is easy. Just follow the steps on the screen or ask a librarian. You can find a book by its title, author, or subject.

Take a Look

FINDING BOOKS IN THE LIBRARY

Each book in the library has a **call number** that indicates its place on the shelves. The call number is on the computer listing. It is also on the spine of the book.

Most books in the library are nonfiction. Nonfiction books give facts. Nonfiction books are on the shelves in call number order.

For more on reference books, see page 34.

The library also has a reference section. This section has encyclopedias, almanacs, and other resources. Reference books also have call numbers. They often start with the letter *R* for *reference*. You cannot take reference books out of the library.

Sometimes you want to find fiction—stories and novels. Books of fiction are on their own shelves.

Olga is looking for a book about *Star Trek*. She found this listing in the computer catalog.

Solow, Herbert F., and Justman, Robert H.   **791.457 S689i**
  Inside Star Trek: The Real Story
Summary: An account of the production of the TV show, Star Trek.

The listing gives the names of the authors. The title of the book—*Inside Star Trek*—is given under the authors. There is a short summary. The number on the right is the call number.

OTHER LIBRARY RESOURCES

There is more to the library than books. They have newspapers and magazines. You can get tapes and videos. Libraries have files filled with information. Many also have resources on computers. Finally, they have librarians. Ask a librarian for help if you are having trouble finding something.

Try It Out

Dale found these book listings on the library computer catalog:

Richards, Jon   **629.47**
Space Vehicles

Summary: Examines different types of machines used in space exploration, including probes, satellites, shuttles, and rockets.

Vogt, Gregory   **629.44**
The Space Shuttle

Summary: An explanation of the Space Shuttle, its parts, and how they function. Describes the pre-flight, launching, flight, and landing.

---

1. What is the call number for the book, *The Space Shuttle*?

   _____

2. Who is the author of *Space Vehicles*? _____

3. Which book would help you learn about launching a

   space shuttle? _____

On Your Own

Visit your library and find two resources about space travel. Only one can be a book. On the following lines, describe these resources.

_____

_____

LESSON 4
Using the Internet

Can you get on-line? Maybe you have a home computer. More and more schools are on-line. Your library may be on-line too.

The resources on the Internet are endless. You can get good information from libraries and museums. Colleges put information on the Internet too. So does the government.

Take a Look

Kyla had to do a report on the planet Mars. She went to the library and got some books. Then she went on-line. First she found a science resource Web site. There Kyla found many links to information on Mars. For example, she found great photos on the NASA Web site.

Finding information on the Internet is easy. All you do is type in a topic in a search engine. The computer searches for it. In a few seconds, it lists sources of information. You click what you want to read.

You have to be careful though. For most topics, there is too much information. You could never look at it all. It would be easy to waste time.

To save time, narrow your topic. Think about exactly what you want. Suppose you want to know about animals that took part in early space flight. The topic *space flight* is too broad. So is *animals*. To narrow the topic, you could type *space flight and animals*. Then you would get more sources you could use.

Try It Out

Four broad topics are listed here. Think of a way to narrow each topic. Write two words you could type to find specific information. Look for something that interests you.

UFOs: _____

automobiles: _____

TV shows: _____

popular music: _____

You can download and print information from the Internet. Be sure to note the Web sites you use. You may have to go back there. If you write a report, you will need to list the sites you used.

Anyone can put information on the Internet. Some sites try to sell things. Others try to persuade you to think a particular way. Not all the information is true.

How can you find a good Web site? Look for ones that are well organized. Does the information seem well researched? Does a college, museum, or government office run the site? If so, you can probably trust it.

On Your Own

Use a computer at school, home, or the library to search the Internet. Search for information on a topic that interests you. On the following lines, write the topic you researched. List three Web sites that you visited to find information on this topic.

Topic: _____

Web sites: _____

_____

_____

_____

Libraries have books about jobs and how to find them. They have information about special job training programs too. Of course, the library also has the local newspapers. The Help Wanted section of the newspaper lists many jobs.

Look at the job listings from the Help Wanted section below. The companies listed have job openings they would like to fill. Most job listings begin by telling you the type of job it is. They also tell you the kinds of hours you would be working. Of course, the phone number and address of the company are also listed. Some job listings will include other requirements as well.

PARKING LOT CASHIER
Monday-Friday, 12-2 pm only.
Apply in person. Centerton
Town Hall, 50 Lincoln Place,
Room 304.

RENTAL AGENT, Busy
real estate agency. Weekends.
Hourly plus commission.
Experience not req'd. Call
Mr. Thomas 555-9877,

RESTAURANT WAITSTAFF,
Weekends only. Apply:
Grandma's Kitchen, 200
Central Avenue, Delyria.

SECRETARY Afternoons,
Wed-Fri, Donegan Law Office.
Word Processing and legal
experience a plus. Fax résumé
to 555-8999.

SECRETARY Spanish/English
Bi-lingual. Gomez Imports.
Experience with word
processing a must. Attractive
surroundings. Call: 555-8787.

SECURITY OFFICER
P/T. Nights. Ideal for added
income. Above-average wages.
Apply: Skyline Security, 422
Washington Street, Daytonville.

For example, Ralph is looking for a job in the Help Wanted section. He wants to buy a car. He is looking for a job that pays well. Between school and basketball, he can only work nights. After looking at the Help Wanted section above, Ralph decides to call Skyline Security. He can work nights and make above-average wages.

YOUR TURN

1. Which company is looking for someone who speaks both Spanish and English?

   _____

2. Which companies are looking for someone to work only on the weekends?

   _____

Chapter Three

REVIEW

You have learned a lot already! Look at the checklist and check off what you have learned. You can add some of your own ideas on the lines following the checklist.

To make the best use of resources for studying, I:

- ☐ use a dictionary to find the spelling, pronunciation, and meaning of a word. (Lessons 1 and 2)

- ☐ use a thesaurus to find synonyms for words. (Lessons 1 and 2)

- ☐ use an encyclopedia to find facts and information about a topic. (Lessons 1 and 2)

- ☐ use atlases to find maps. (Lesson 1)

- ☐ use almanacs to find up-to-date facts. (Lesson 1)

- ☐ use newspapers and magazines to find up-to-date information. (Lesson 1)

- ☐ use the computer catalog in the library to find books. (Lesson 3)

- ☐ use the call number to find books on the shelf. (Lesson 3)

- ☐ search for information on the Internet. (Lesson 4)

- ☐ narrow the topics I search for on the Internet. (Lesson 4)

- ☐ look for Web sites I can trust when I search for information on the Internet. (Lesson 4)

- ☐ _____

- ☐ _____

CHAPTER THREE PRACTICE

Answer the following items about what you have learned in this chapter.

1. Which book would you use to find each thing? Write *dictionary*, *thesaurus*, or *encyclopedia*.

    a. another word for *sad* _____

    b. how to pronounce *petite* _____

    c. the early history of Delaware _____

    d. the meaning of *blatant* _____

    e. a synonym for *take* _____

    f. facts about the planet Mars _____

2. Use this dictionary entry to answer the following questions.

    feign (FAYN) *v.* To pretend

    a. What is the meaning of *feign*? _____

    b. What part of speech is *feign*? _____

    c. Does *feign* rhyme with *lean*, *pain*, or *sign*? _____

3. Which resource would you use to find each of these things? Write *atlas*, *almanac*, or *magazine*.

    a. a map showing roads in Canada _____

    b. what Congress did last month _____

    c. who won Oscars last year _____

4. Read this listing from a library computer catalog. Use it to answer the questions.

> **Fry, Ronald W.   371.302FRY**
> *Last Minute Study Tips*
> Summary: Discusses a variety of simple ways to improve study habits.

   a. What is the title of this book? _____

   b. What is the call number? _____

   c. Who is the author? _____

5. Alfredo wants to check out a book with the call number 808.32 G23. Circle the section of the library where he will find it.

   reference section   nonfiction section   fiction section

6. Circle the topic in each group that is *most* narrow.

   a. dairy products   making cottage cheese   cheeses

   b. the American   settling California   the California
      West   gold rush

   c. reptiles   turtles   snapping turtles

   d. the Susan B. Anthony   U.S. coins   U.S. silver dollars
      silver dollar

Talk It Over

With a group of classmates, talk about what you have learned. Answer these questions:

▶ What is the most interesting fact you learned about space exploration?

▶ What does the word *trajectory* mean?

chapter three

LEARNING STYLES CHECK-IN

Check off the ways you learn best. Then use the suggestions to help you learn more about study resources.

☐ **Sound-smart learner**

- Talk to a librarian about resources. Ask questions about how to use reference books and computers.

☐ **People-smart learner**

- E-mail people in your class. Talk about useful on-line resources you have found.

☐ **Self-smart learner**

- List some problems you have had using resources. Write some daily or short-term goals that will help you get better at using them.

☐ **Picture-smart learner**

- Draw pictures of a dictionary, thesaurus, and encyclopedia. Each time you use one, list what you were looking for.

- Look for pictures in reference books you use. What information do they give?

☐ **Action-smart learner**

- Walk through your local or school library. What resources do you see? Try using them.

☐ **Word-smart learner**

- Use the dictionary and thesaurus often. Try to find the exact words that express your ideas.

- Look at different dictionaries and encyclopedias. Which do you like more? Which would be best for you?

☐ **Number-smart learner**

- Make flow charts that show how to use study resources. One chart can show how to use the Internet. Another can be for the library computer catalog.

Chapter
FOUR

Understanding What You Read

BIANCA'S STRUGGLE

Bianca has to read Chapter 3 of her social studies book. She opens the book to page 118. The topic is the Maya people of Central America. Bianca knows nothing about this topic.

While reading, Bianca says each word aloud. By the time she finishes the second paragraph, Bianca is restless. She gets up and stretches. She sits down. Where had she stopped? She cannot remember. So she goes back to the beginning.

In the fourth paragraph, Bianca sees the words **hieroglyphic writing** in boldface type. "What's that?" she wonders aloud.

Bianca reaches page 119. There are only 24 pages to go. She leafs through the chapter. She sees a picture of a pyramid in a beautiful jungle. Bianca wishes she were there.

It is getting late. Bianca has to answer the questions on page 144. She cannot find the answers. So she guesses.

What happened? Bianca tried to read the assignment. She did not have the right skills. Bianca needs to become a more active reader. In this chapter, you will learn skills that will help you use your textbooks. These skills will help you understand what you read.

What Do You Think?

▶ What advice do you have for Bianca to improve her reading?
▶ What do you do to make sure you understand a reading assignment?

LESSON 1
How to Get the Most Out of Your Textbooks

Have you ever moved to a new house or apartment? You probably wanted to know how to make the most of your new home. It is important to make the most of your new textbooks too. Different parts of the books will help you in different ways.

Take a Look

At the front of a textbook, you will find the table of contents. The table of contents lists the units and chapters in the book. It tells you what you will be reading.

Your textbook has a glossary too. It is at the back. The glossary lists key words. It gives their meanings too.

The index is also at the back. The index lists every topic in the book. It also gives the pages that tell about each topic.

Try It Out

Use this part of a table of contents from a social studies textbook to answer the following questions:

TABLE OF CONTENTS

CHAPTER 1   The Geography of the United States 1-27
CHAPTER 2   The Cultures of the First Americans 28-59
CHAPTER 3   The Spanish Reach the Americas 60-89
CHAPTER 4   The Africans Reach the Americas 90-107

---

1. Which chapter tells about the cultures of Native Americans?

   _____

2. Which pages in the book tell about Africans reaching America?

   _____

Use this part of a glossary from a social studies textbook to answer the questions below.

GLOSSARY

adobe bricks made of sun-dried clay (p. 270)

annex to add into a nation (p. 178)

arsenal a place where weapons are stored (p. 217)

assimilate to absorb someone into or make someone part of a culture or society (p. 287)

---

3. What is the meaning of *annex*? _____

4. On which page in the book is the word *adobe* used? _____

Use this part of an index from a social studies textbook to answer the questions below.

INDEX

Nationalism, 167-168
Native Americans
   and British Colonists, 55-56
   and Columbus, 27-29, 33
   contributions to American culture 48-49

eastern woodlands people, 19
of Great Plains, 258-267
of Latin America 7-15
reservations, 260-263
Navigation Acts, 87

---

5. Which pages tell about the Native Americans of the Great

   Plains? _____

6. Which pages tell about the reservation system? _____

On Your Own

Use your own social studies or science book to answer these questions.

1. On what page does Chapter 3 begin? _____

2. List three words beginning with *B* in the glossary.

   _____ _____ _____

3. What is the first index entry? _____

LESSON 2
More on Active Reading

How do you choose what to watch on TV? Lots of people surf the channels. That way they get an overview of what is on. Then they settle down to watch one show. Reading a textbook is similar.

Take a Look

Whenever you sit down to read from your textbook, skim through the whole assignment. Only read the important parts. That gives you an overview of the assignment.

What are the most important parts? You should read the title and headings. They show what the section is all about. Also read the first sentence of each paragraph. It usually gives the main idea. Take a look at the key words in boldface type. You need to know them. Finally, look over the questions at the end. They cover important information.

Once you have skimmed an assignment, it is time to read it in detail. Go back to the beginning. Read every word. You should also:

- Write the meanings of the key words in your notebook.
- Write your own questions for each section.
- Answer your own questions.
- Answer the questions at the end of the assignment.

Try It Out

Read this section from a social studies textbook on the top of the next page. Then answer the questions that follow the section.

Early People of the Southwest.
In the hot, dry Southwest, many people lived in villages. They farmed beans, corn, and squash. Often they had to dig canals to bring river water to their fields.

Some of the groups were great builders. The Anasazi, for example, built villages into the sides of cliffs. They lived in buildings made of mud bricks called **adobe** (ah-DOH-bee). Some of these buildings had 800 rooms.

Life was hard in the villages on cliffs. Sometimes, there was a **drought** (drowt), or a period of dry weather. Droughts caused the crops to die. During a drought, many people also died.

1. Write the heading of this section.

   _____

   _____

2. Write the key words in this section and write their meanings.

   _____

   _____

   _____

3. Write a question of your own about this section. Then answer it.

   _____

   _____

   _____

   _____

On Your Own

Skim a section of one of your own textbooks. On a separate sheet of paper, write the heading or headings of the section. Then write the key words and their meanings. Finally, write your own question about the section.

LESSON 3
Using SQ3R

Key Term

SQ3R a way to actively read textbooks

SQ3R is a good way to actively read textbooks. It stands for Survey, Question, Read, Record, and Review.

Take a Look

Survey: Skim through the text you will read. Read the titles, headings, and key words. Get a good overview.

Question: Ask yourself questions about this reading. If a chapter has questions, read them. Think about what you want to learn as you read.

Read: Read the pages carefully. Look for the main ideas. Try to answer the questions you have asked.

Record: Take notes on the reading. Write down the main ideas and key terms. Also note important names and dates.

Review: Look over your notes. Make sure they are all there. Sum up what you have learned.

In Lesson 2, you learned how to *survey* and *question* a chapter or section of a textbook. Now it's time to *read* the chapter. Read slowly and you are likely to remember more. In your notebook, you will *record* notes. After reading, *review* your notes. Reviewing is a way to make sure you have all the important points.

How do you know what questions to ask before you read? Textbook chapters have titles and headings. You can rewrite them as questions. Look at this chapter title, "Native Americans Build Great Empires." You could rewrite it this way, "What great empires did Native Americans build?" Then try to answer the question as you read.

Active readers understand what they read. Here are some do's and don'ts to help you become an active reader.

 Do

- Set realistic reading goals. Try not to read too much at once.
- See words as parts of phrases, not single words.
- Think about what the author says. Guess what will come next.

 Don't

- Read aloud to yourself. Saying each word slows you down.
- Use a finger to point at words. It will slow you down too.
- Skip over important words. Take time to look them up!

Try It Out

Here are some headings from a social studies textbook. Rewrite each one as a question.

1. "The Plains People and the Buffalo"

   _____

2. "The Iroquois Form the League of Five Nations"

   _____

3. "The Remarkable City of Tenochtitlán"

   _____

On Your Own

On the lines, write about a problem you have when reading. What can you do to solve it?

_____

_____

_____

Reading helps in most areas of life. For example, in the grocery store, it is important to read the labels on products. The label on a food package lists the **ingredients**—what is in the food.

Food labels also give nutrition facts. The label tells the size of a serving. It lists how many servings are in the package. It also tells about the nutrients in the food. Nutrients, like fat, protein, and carbohydrates, are parts of food. Your body needs nutrients to stay healthy.

Check the nutrition facts on prepared foods before you buy. Avoid foods that are high in fat and sodium.

NUTRITION FACTS	
Serving Size 1 cup (239G)	
Servings Per Container 2	
Amount Per Serving	
Calories 90 Calories from Fat 20	
% Daily Value*	
Total Fat 2g	3%
Saturated Fat	3%
Polyunsaturated 0g	
Monounsaturated 1g	
Cholesterol 20mg	7%
Sodium 870mg	36%
Total Carbohydrate 13g	4%
Dietary Fiber 2g	8%
Sugars 0g	
Protein 6g	
Vitamin A 30% · Vitamin C	0%
Calcium 2% · Iron 4%	

* Percent Daily Values are based on a 2,000 calorie diet

INGREDIENTS: Water, Chicken, Rice, Chicken Broth, Celery, Salt

HOME CHICKEN & WILD RI
MADE WITH 100% CHICK

For example, Jodi is going shopping. She wants to buy soup that has less than 50 mg of cholesterol per serving. She looks at the label to find out how much cholesterol is in this soup. She sees that it only has 20 mg of cholesterol per serving. She decides to buy the soup.

YOUR TURN

1. What is the serving size of the soup? _____

2. How many calories are in one serving? _____

Chapter Four

REVIEW

You have learned a lot already! Look at the checklist and check off what you have learned.

To better understand what I read, I:

☐ look over the table of contents of each textbook I use. (Lesson 1)

☐ use the glossary to check the meanings of words. (Lesson 1)

☐ use the index to find topics in a textbook. (Lesson 1)

☐ read the chapter title to know what the chapter is about. (Lesson 1)

☐ read each section heading to find out what a section is about. (Lesson 2)

☐ make sure I know the meanings of key words in boldface type. (Lesson 2)

☐ skim the whole reading assignment before reading in detail. (Lesson 2)

☐ read the first sentence of each paragraph to find out the main ideas. (Lesson 2)

☐ read each assignment in detail after skimming it. (Lesson 2)

☐ answer my own questions and the questions in the text. (Lesson 2)

☐ use the SQ3R way to read textbooks. (Lesson 3)

☐ use the chapter titles and section headings to form questions for myself. (Lesson 3)

☐ work to become a fast, active reader. (Lesson 3)

CHAPTER FOUR PRACTICE

Answer the following items about what you have learned in this chapter.

1. Which part of a textbook would you use to find each thing? Write *table of contents, index,* or *glossary.*

   a. to see how many chapters are in the book _____

   b. to learn the meaning of *lava* _____

   c. to find out if the textbook tells about earthquakes

   _____

   d. to learn what pages tell about Martin Luther King, Jr.

   _____

   e. to see where Chapter 4 begins and ends _____

   f. to check the meaning of a key word _____

2. Read this section from a science textbook. Then answer the questions that follow.

   SCIENCE

   Animals in Winter.
   Many animals do not migrate in winter. They have other ways to survive the cold. Some animals go into a deep sleep called **hibernation.**

   During hibernation, an animal's body temperature drops. It drops to about the freezing point of water. Breathing, heartbeat, and other body activities become very slow in a hibernating animal.

   ---

   a. What is the heading of the section? _____

   b. What is the key word and what is its meaning?

   _____

3. Check the four things you should do when skimming a chapter.

_____ Read the titles and headings.

_____ Read the first sentence of each paragraph.

_____ Take good notes on every paragraph.

_____ Read the questions at the end of the chapter.

_____ Read every word in the chapter.

_____ Take a look at the key words.

4. Here are the steps of the SQ3R method. They are out of order. Write them in the correct order that you would use to study.

Read   Question   Review   Survey   Record

a. _____

b. _____

c. _____

d. _____

e. _____

5. Write three things you can do to become a faster and more active reader.

a. _____

b. _____

c. _____

Talk It Over

With a group of classmates, talk about what you have learned. Answer these questions:

▶ Why is it a good idea to skim chapter titles?

▶ When should you use an index?

chapter four

LEARNING STYLES CHECK-IN

Check off the ways you learn best. Then use the suggestions to help you understand what you read.

Sound-smart learner

- Tape-record the questions you ask yourself as you read an assignment. Then, after you read, play back your questions and answer them.

People-smart learner

- Stage an SQ3R demonstration. Show other students how to use this method.

Self-smart learner

- Make your own list of do's and don'ts for becoming an active reader. Post them in your study space. Try to follow them when you study.

Picture-smart learner

- Pay attention to photos, charts, and diagrams in textbooks.
- Draw diagrams and sketches to sum up what you read in social studies and science.

Action-smart learner

- When you read science, do experiments to show the main ideas.
- When you read social studies, act out famous events.

Word-smart learner

- Write your own chapter titles and section headings for your textbooks. How are they different from the ones in the book?
- Read over the answers you write to study questions. See if you can write a clearer, better answer in fewer words.

Number-smart learner

- Measure the speed of your reading. How many words can you read in a minute? Do you read science or social studies faster? How fast can you read and still understand the material well?

Chapter
FIVE

Note Taking in Class

SHANNON AND JACQUES

Look at how these two students take notes.

Shannon tries to write every word the teacher says. Most of the time, her head is down. She has to write so fast that she cannot think about what the teacher says. By the end of class, her fingers hurt. Sometimes she fills six pages with notes. When it comes time to study, she reads all the notes. Often they do not make much sense. Getting through them is not easy.

Jacques also takes notes in class. However, he watches the teacher. He listens carefully. He tries to figure out what is important. Then he writes down the important points. Jacques's notes may only fill half a page. Everything he writes, however, is usually on the tests.

What happened? Jacques is taking better notes. He does not have as many notes as Shannon. His notes cover the most important points though. Jacques thinks as he takes notes. So he probably learns more. His notes are useful when he studies for a test.

What Do You Think?

▶ Why is it important to take notes in class?

▶ How do you decide what notes to take?

LESSON 1
Taking Notes in Class

It is not enough to sit in class. You have to be ready to learn.

Take a Look

Here are some tips for getting ready:

- Sit up. Sitting up comfortably makes it easier to pay attention.

- Keep your eyes and ears on the teacher. If you watch and listen carefully, you are more likely to understand.

- Avoid distractions. Learning is serious. Try not to crack jokes, stare out the window, or whisper with friends.

- Take notes. Taking notes in class is the best way to learn and remember information.

Look at the students in the drawing below.

As you can see, these students are not ready to learn. One student is not sitting up. Another is being distracted by a friend. None of the students are taking notes.

Taking notes in class will help you learn. You cannot copy everything though. As your teacher speaks, you have to decide what is most important.

These tips will help you tell what is most important.

- Know your teachers. Your teachers may say important things louder. They may raise a finger to point out a main idea. Teachers often write important ideas on the board in large letters.

- Listen for phrases that show something is important. *First of all*, *most important*, *to sum up*, and *finally* are examples. They signal important points.

- Ask yourself questions during class. For example, "Do I understand this information?" If you do, great! If not, ask a question. Write your question and answer in your notes.

Try It Out

Complete each sentence below.

1. To decide what notes to take, I should listen for _____

   _____

2. I should also watch for _____

   _____

3. I should ask myself _____

   _____

On Your Own

Work with a friend. Compare your notes for a recent class with your friend's notes. How are the notes the same? How are the notes different? How could your notes be better? On the lines below, write what you find.

_____

_____

_____

_____

_____

LESSON 2
Listening for Signal Phrases and Key Words

Key Term

signal phrase phrase that tells you something important is about to come

Suppose you could only save three things from your house. Chances are you would take the most valuable, important things.

In class, you cannot note everything the teacher says. You have to choose the important things. One way is to listen for signal phrases.

Take a Look

Signal phrases tell that something important is about to come. Some common signal phrases are *first of all*, *most important*, *to sum up*, and *therefore*.

In your notes, write the point that comes after a signal phrase. Find a way to show that this information is important. You might put a star next to it. You might write it a little bigger.

Colin's teacher told the class:

> "People enjoy tasting food, listening to music, touching things, smelling flowers, and watching movies. These activities are possible because of the sense organs: skin, eyes, ears, tongue, and nose. These sense organs do more than help you enjoy the world. Most important, they constantly send information to the brain that helps you survive."

Colin's notes are shown below.

> Sense organs—constantly send important information to brain.

What signal phrase did Colin hear? _____

Some words your teacher uses are very important too. They are key words. Usually you have to learn the meanings of key words.

Teachers often say these key words a little louder. They will tell you the meaning of the key words. They might write them on the board. You should write key words in your notes. Write their meanings too.

Try It Out

Colin's teacher also told the class:

> "Everything you see is light. Suppose you are looking at a car. Light bounces off the car and enters your **pupil**. That's the black opening at the center of your eye. From there the 'light information' travels to your brain. Then you know you are seeing a car."

Write the key word and its meaning on the following lines.

_____

_____

On Your Own

A teacher told his class:

> "First of all, much of what you believe to be taste is really smell. If you doubt it, think about the last time you had a head cold and stuffy nose. It was almost impossible to taste your food. Smells are picked up by special cells in the nose. These cells have **cilia**. Cilia are hairlike structures that are connected to nerves. The cilia pass smells along to the brain."

Take notes on the lines below. Remember the importance of signal words. You should also write down key words.

_____

_____

_____

LESSON 3
Using Abbreviations and Signs

Suppose you had to send a letter to California. Would you use the abbreviation CA? Would you write California? In math, do you use the % sign? Or, do you write out percent? Most people use abbreviations and signs to save time.

Take a Look

Sign	Meaning
w/	with
+	and, also
>	greater than
<	less than
$	money
↑	increasing
↓	decreasing
∴	therefore
esp.	especially
*	very important
#	number

Abbreviations make note taking easier. You can make up your own abbreviations. One way is to leave out the vowels of a word. The vowels are *a*, *e*, *i*, *o*, and *u*. You can also leave out little words like *the*, *a*, and *in*.

Signs stand for words or groups of words. You know some signs from math and everyday life. To the left are some common signs and their meanings. You can use them in your notes to save time.

Jonni's teacher told her class one day:

> "Put your hand in the middle of your chest. There you will find your heart, the hardest-working organ in your body. It beats between 60 and 80 times a minute. Each day it pumps about 2000 gallons of blood. This workhorse is about the size of your fist."

Here are the notes Jonni took. Jonni used abbreviations and left small words out.

♥ = hardest working organ
60-80 hrtbts/min.
pumps 2000 gal/day
about size of fist

Try It Out

Here are the notes Tawana wrote from a science class:

Have one pint blood per 12 lbs body wght

55% of bld = plasma, 93% of plsma = H2O

Bld's 2 main roles: 1st: carry food, O2 2nd: fight infection

What signs and abbreviations did Tawana use? Write the meanings of three signs and three abbreviations.

Abbreviation   Meaning

_____   _____

_____   _____

_____   _____

Sign   Meaning

_____   _____

_____   _____

_____   _____

On Your Own

Take notes on this information. Use abbreviations and signs. Write your notes on the following lines.

The largest part of the brain is the cerebrum. It makes up more than 80 percent of the brain. It is divided into a right half and a left half. The cerebrum controls thinking and memory.

_____

_____

_____

_____

LESSON 4
What to Do With Your Notes at Home

What do you do after you shoot a roll of film? You get the film developed. That is the only way to see the pictures.

Something similar should happen when you take notes. You have to develop them at home. That will give you a good picture of what you need to know.

Take a Look

How should you develop your notes? First, read over them. Do that as soon as possible. That way, the information is still fresh in your mind. Decide whether anything is unclear. If your notes are hard to read, you might copy them. If you used abbreviations and signs, you might write out the full words. That will help you learn the information better.

Pak took these notes in his science class:

cerebrum—imprtnt prt of brain

80 %/ rt 1/2, lft 1/2; thnkng, mem.

At home, he read them over. The notes were okay, but he wanted to develop them. So, Pak rewrote the notes to fill in what he had left out.

Cerebrum=most important part of brain;

makes up 80% of brain; has left half and right half;

cerebrum controls thinking and memory

Sometimes you might find gaps in your notes. You can fill them in at home. You can look up missing information in a textbook or other source. You can check a friend's notes. It is a good idea to leave a little extra space when you take notes.

Sometimes you may find something in your notes that does not make sense. Do not ignore it! Ask your teacher about it.

Try It Out

Read Didi's notes. Didi took them in science.

human brain 3lbs., only 2% of body wght

uses 20% of body O2, can go 3-5 min. w/o O2

1. Develop Didi's notes on the following lines. Fill in the gaps.

_____

_____

2. Write a question Didi might need to ask about something unclear.

_____

After you develop your notes, read them over every so often. When it is time to study for a test, reread your notes.

On Your Own

1. On the following lines, list some ways that you can take and develop better notes.

_____

_____

2. Explain why note taking will help you succeed in school.

_____

_____

In your notes, abbreviations save time and space. The Help Wanted pages of the newspaper also use abbreviations. Abbreviations let people list their ads in less space.

In order to read the Help Wanted pages, you will need to figure out abbreviations. These job ads have abbreviations. Think about what they mean.

For example, Keisha is looking for a job. She looks at the first ad and sees the abbreviations. Before she goes any further, she makes sure she understands the abbreviations. She figures out the following:

F/T = full time

perm. = permanent

Min. 3 yrs. exp. = minimum 3 years experience

COOK, F/T, perm. Min. 3 yrs exp. Nicole's Restaurant, 472 Seward St. Apply in person.

DENTAL ASST. w/exp. 4 days, exc. sal./bnfts. Highbridge Dental Center. 555-9801

DRIVERS, F/T and P/T. Jun.-Sept. Ice cream truck. Neat apprnce. Ding-Dong Ice Cream Co. 555-1876.

DRY CLEANING & SHIRT PRESSER, Exp. re'q. A-1 Dry Cleaners, 55 Langdon Court, New Delphi.

GRNDSKPR. Yr-rnd. Exp. prfrd. Must have clean drvrs lic. Sugar Hill Country Club. 555-9099.

YOUR TURN

1. Look at the second ad. Tell what you think each abbreviation means.

   w/exp. _____

   exc. sal./bnfts. _____

2. Look at the third ad. Tell what you think each abbreviation means.

   F/T. and P/T. _____

   Jun.-Sept. _____

3. Look at the last ad. Tell what you think each abbreviation means.

   GRNDSKPR. _____

   Yr-rnd. _____

Chapter Five

REVIEW

You have learned a lot already! Look at the checklist and check off what you have learned.

When I take notes in class, I:

☐ sit up and pay attention in class. (Lesson 1)

☐ take notes on the most important information. (Lesson 1)

☐ listen for signal phrases that lead up to important information. (Lesson 2)

☐ show important points in my notes by using a star or large letters. (Lesson 2)

☐ listen for key words that I need to learn. (Lesson 2)

☐ copy key words and their meanings into my notes. (Lesson 2)

☐ use abbreviations in my notes to save time and space. (Lesson 3)

☐ use signs in my notes to save time and space. (Lesson 3)

☐ read my notes soon after class. (Lesson 4)

☐ develop my notes by copying anything that is unclear. (Lesson 4)

☐ fill in any gaps in my notes. (Lesson 4)

☐ ask questions if I do not understand something in my notes. (Lesson 4)

Answer the following items about what you have learned in Chapter 5.

1. Place a check next to four things you should do in class to be ready to learn.

    _____ **a.** Listen for key words and signal phrases.

    _____ **b.** Whisper and chat with friends.

    _____ **c.** Sit up comfortably.

    _____ **d.** Keep your eyes on your desk.

    _____ **e.** Finish up your homework.

    _____ **f.** Take notes.

    _____ **g.** Ask yourself questions about what you hear.

2. Read this paragraph. Write the signal phrase on the following lines. Then write the important point that follows the signal phrase.

    > Salt can be removed from sea water. This is called desalination. The salt taken from sea water has many uses. Most important, desalination makes fresh water for drinking.

    _____

    _____

    _____

3. Read this paragraph. Write the key word and its meaning.

> Metals are among our most useful resources. Metals must be separated from the **ores** they are found with in the ground. An ore is a rock from which metals can be gotten.

_____

_____

4. Write five signs you might use in your notes on the right side below. Write what each sign means on the line next to it.

a. _____   _____

b. _____   _____

c. _____   _____

d. _____   _____

e. _____   _____

5. Take notes on these sentences. See how many abbreviations you can use.

> Thomas Jefferson of Virginia wrote the Declaration of Independence. The Continental Congress approved the Declaration in Philadelphia, Pennsylvania, on July 4, 1776.

_____

_____

_____

_____

chapter five

LEARNING STYLES CHECK-IN

Check off the ways you learn best. Then use the suggestions to help you take and use notes in class.

Word-smart learner

- Develop your notes into short paragraphs. Sum up the important ideas as clearly as possible.
- Speak up in class. Find interesting ways to state the ideas in your notes.

Sound-smart learner

- Listen carefully to your teacher's voice. He or she might say the most important points in a special tone of voice.

People-smart learner

- Compare notes with a friend. Check to see if you both have the same main points.
- Use your notes in a study group with three or four classmates.

Self-smart learner

- Work hard at developing your notes at home. Use a textbook or other source to make sure you have all the important points covered.

Picture-smart learner

- Draw illustrations of some of your notes. A picture can be worth a thousand words.
- Make up your own signs to use in notes.

Action-smart learner

- Notice how your teachers stress important ideas. Do they wave a finger or arm? Do they tense up?

Number-smart learner

- Use charts and outlines to keep your notes in order.

Chapter
SIX

Note Taking From Textbooks

KELLY TRIES NOTE TAKING

Kelly wants to do better in social studies this year. She reads the assignments each week. She answers the questions at the end of the chapter too. Even so, her first test did not go very well. It seemed as if there was just too much information to remember. On the day of the test, she just could not remember a lot of information.

To prepare for her second test, Kelly tried taking notes on each chapter she read. She was not sure how to do it though. For one thing, her notes got jumbled up and confused. Sometimes she felt as if she were copying the whole book! Unfortunately, her grade on the second test was not much better than the first.

What should Kelly do? Believe it or not, Kelly is on the right track. Taking notes as you read is a key to success in class and on tests. However, it is also important to take the right notes and organize them well.

What Do You Think?

▶ Do you take notes from your textbooks as you read? How do you decide what to put in your notes?

▶ Are your notes organized? What do you use to organize them?

LESSON 1
Noting Main Ideas and Details

Key Term
main idea the most important point in a reading passage

Do you want to get better grades on tests and save yourself study time too? Then try taking notes. Good notes are the best way to learn and remember the **main ideas** and important details that you read.

Main ideas are the most important points in a reading passage. To find the main ideas, ask: "What does the author most want me to learn?"

Details are facts and examples that tell about a main idea. To find important details, ask: "What information proves the main idea?"

Take a Look
Read this paragraph. The notes show the main idea and details.

> Michael Jordan was one of the world's most successful athletes ever. A guard for the Chicago Bulls, Jordan won four Most Valuable Player awards in the NBA. He is the third highest scorer in basketball history. His on-court talent and will to win attracted countless fans. In 1997, Michael Jordan earned over $78 million.

Main Idea: Michael Jordan was one of the world's most successful athletes.

Detail: Jordan won four MVP awards in NBA.

Detail: Jordan is the third-highest scorer in basketball history.

Detail: Jordan earned over $78 million in 1997.

Try It Out

Now read the second paragraph about Michael Jordan.

> Michael Jordan had a long history of winning. In high school, he was most valuable player several years running. In 1982, he led the University of North Carolina to the NCAA title. Jordan was named Player of the Year in college basketball in 1984. That same year, he won an Olympic gold medal. Then in 1985 Jordan entered the pros and was Rookie of the Year.

The main idea of this paragraph is shown below. Take notes that show the important details.

Main Idea: _Michael Jordan had a long history of winning._ _____

Detail: _____

Detail: _____

Detail: _____

Detail: _____

Detail: _____

On Your Own

On a separate sheet of paper, take notes on this paragraph. If you are unsure about what your notes should look like, review the Take A Look and Try It Out sections

> In 1993, Michael Jordan left basketball for baseball. Jordan played for minor league teams in Alabama and Arizona. Changing sports wasn't easy for the 31-year-old Jordan. So everyone was happy when Jordan returned to basketball—and the Chicago Bulls—in 1995.

LESSON 2
Notes in a Pyramid

Key Term

note pyramid a drawing to help you organize your thoughts

Your notes should always keep the main ideas separate from the details. If the main ideas and details get mixed up, notes are less useful.

A **note pyramid** is one way to organize your notes. Write the main ideas at the top. List important details in the middle. At the tip, write a point that sums up the whole paragraph or passage.

Take a Look

Here is how one student used a note pyramid to show her notes for the paragraph about Michael Jordan.

Michael Jordan was one of the world's most successful athletes ever. A guard for the Chicago Bulls, Jordan won four Most Valuable Player awards in the NBA. He is the third highest scorer in basketball history. His on-court talent and will to win attracted countless fans. In 1997, Michael Jordan earned over $78 million.

Main Idea: Michael Jordan was probably the most successful athlete of all.

Detail: Jordan is third highest scorer in history.

Detail: Jordan won four MVP awards.

Detail: MJ earns over $78 million.

Point: Michael is a superstar!

Try It Out

Complete the note pyramid for the second paragraph about
Michael Jordan.

> Michael Jordan had a long history of winning. In high school, he was most valuable player several years running. In 1982, he led the University of North Carolina to the NCAA title. Jordan was named Player of the Year in college basketball in 1984. That same year, he won an Olympic gold medal. Then in 1985, Jordan entered the pros and was Rookie of the Year.

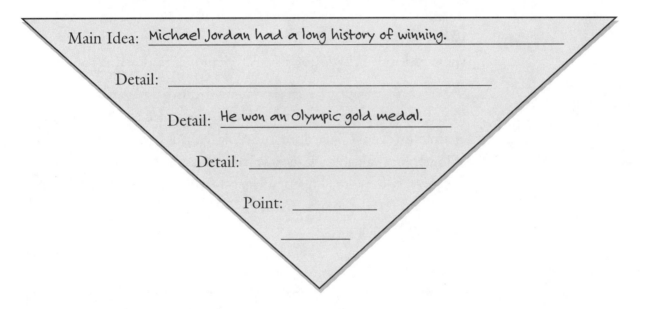

Main Idea: Michael Jordan had a long history of winning.

Detail: _____

Detail: He won an Olympic gold medal.

Detail: _____

Point: _____

_____

On Your Own

On a separate piece of paper, draw a note pyramid of your own.
Use it to take notes on this paragraph.

> In 1993, Michael Jordan left basketball for baseball. Jordan played for minor league teams in Alabama and Arizona. Changing sports wasn't easy for the 31-year-old Jordan. So everyone was happy when Jordan returned to basketball—and the Chicago Bulls—in 1995.

LESSON 3

Notes in a Word Web

Key Term

word web a way to organize notes graphically

A **word web** is another handy way to take notes. To begin a web, write the main idea in a circle. Then write important details in boxes around the circle. Draw lines between the circle and the boxes to show how they are linked. Add pictures, symbols, whatever you like!

Take a Look

The word web below shows one student's notes for this paragraph.

> Michael Jordan was one of the world's most successful athletes ever. A guard for the Chicago Bulls, Jordan won four Most Valuable Player awards. He is the third highest scorer in basketball history. His on-court talent and will to win attracted countless fans. In 1997, Michael Jordan earned over $78 million.

Detail: Won 4 MVP awards.

Detail: Earned over $78 million in 1997.

Main Idea: Michael Jordan was one of the world's most successful athletes.

Detail: Attracts countless fans.

Detail: Third highest scorer in basketball history.

Try It Out

This next paragraph tells more about Michael Jordan. As you read, take notes to complete the word web below.

> Michael Jordan had a long history of winning. In high school, he was most valuable player several years running. In 1982, he led the University of North Carolina to the NCAA title. Jordan was named Player of the Year in college basketball in 1984. That same year, he won an Olympic gold medal. Then in 1985, Jordan entered the pros and was Rookie of the Year.

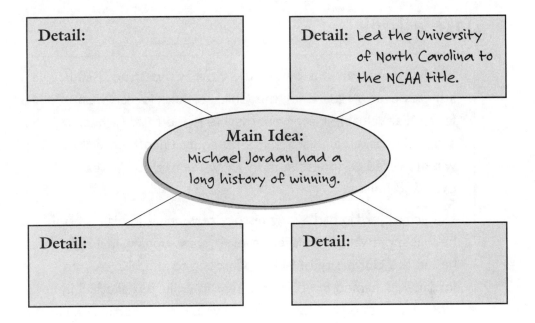

Detail:

Detail: Led the University of North Carolina to the NCAA title.

Main Idea: Michael Jordan had a long history of winning.

Detail:

Detail:

On Your Own

Read the final paragraph about Jordan. On a separate sheet of paper, create your own word web to show the main idea and important details.

> In 1993, Michael Jordan left basketball for baseball. Jordan played for minor league teams in Alabama and Arizona. Changing sports wasn't easy for the 31-year-old Jordan. So everyone was happy when Jordan returned to basketball— and the Chicago Bulls—in 1995.

LESSON 4
Filling Out an Outline

Key Term

outline a way to organize notes

An **outline** is probably the most common way to organize notes. In a way, an outline is like a skeleton. Your notes flesh it out. How? Write the main ideas on lines with Roman numerals. Write the details that tell about a main idea below on lines with capital letters.

Take a Look

> Michael Jordan was one of the world's most successful athletes ever. A guard for the Chicago Bulls, Jordan won four Most Valuable Player awards. He is the third highest scorer in basketball history. His on-court talent and will to win attracted countless fans. In 1997, Michael Jordan earned over $78 million.
>
> Michael Jordan had a long history of winning. In high school, he was most valuable player several years running. In 1982, he led the University of North Carolina to the NCAA title. Jordan was named Player of the Year in college basketball in 1984. That same year, he won an Olympic gold medal. Then in 1985, Jordan entered the pros and was Rookie of the Year.

This outline shows the notes about Michael Jordan.

I. Michael Jordan was one of the world's most successful athletes.

    A. Jordan has won four MVP awards in NBA.

    B. Jordan is the third-highest scorer in basketball history.

    C. Jordan earned over $78 million in 1997.

II. _Michael Jordan had a long history of winning._

    A. _Jordan led UNC to 1982 NCAA title._

    B. _Named Player of the Year in college basketball in 1984._

    C. _Jordan named Rookie of the Year in pros in 1985._

Try It Out

Complete the outline for the paragraph about Michael Jordan.

> In 1993, Michael Jordan left basketball for baseball. Jordan played for minor league teams in Alabama and Arizona. Changing sports wasn't easy for the 31-year-old Jordan. So everyone was happy when Jordan returned to basketball— and the Chicago Bulls—in 1995.

I. _____

    A. _Jordan played minor league baseball in Alabama and Arizona._

    B. _____

    C. _____

On Your Own

On a separate sheet of paper, make an outline to take notes on this paragraph.

> Michael Jordan's return made the Bulls a strong team again. In his fourth game back, Jordan scored 34 points. In his fifth game, he scored 55 points! Without Jordan in 1995, the Bulls had a record of 34–31. With Michael playing, they were 13–4. By 1996, the Bulls had won another NBA title and Jordan was Most Valuable Player again. What a rebound!

LESSON 5
More Note-Taking Styles

There are many ways to take notes. You should use the note-taking style that works best for you. Here are some other note-taking styles to try.

1. **Wired for Sound.** Do you learn best by hearing? If so, a tape recorder can be your notebook. As you read, tape the main ideas and details you want to remember. When it's time to study, hit Play!

2. **Colors and Shapes.** If color catches your eye, use colored pens or pencils for your notes. For example, you might use bright red for main ideas. Then write details in blue or green. You can also change the size of your writing for notes. Write the main ideas in big letters. Details can be smaller.

3. **Musical Notes.** The purpose of notes is to help you remember. If you like music, write some rhyming notes. Then sing the rhyme or jingle to remember something important for a test.

4. **Picture the Notes.** If you like to draw, you can often use a sketch or diagram to grab the main ideas and details. Be creative. The sketch below shows Michael Jordan. The sketch shows how he makes a lot of money.

5. **Shortcut Notes.** Our world is filled with signs and symbols— # $? ! ↓ ÷ ♥. You can use symbols from math, sports, and everyday life. They will make taking notes easier since you do not have to write as much. Using symbols also shows that you understand the ideas in a passage.

6. **Note Cards.** Three-by-five cards will help you get a grip on your notes. You can write one main idea and its supporting details on each card. To study, all you have to do is flip through your cards.

In the end, you have to decide which note-taking style is best for you. Experiment and have fun with the different suggestions. One or more is sure to work for you.

On Your Own

Before your next test, organize your notes using at least three of the note-taking methods you just learned. If one method does not seem to work for you, choose a different method.

Tina just got a job at Value Video. On her first day at work, the store manager gave her an employee's manual and told her to read it. Tina brought it home and began to read it. She took notes to help her remember what she read.

VALUE VIDEO HANDBOOK   1
_____

- All employees at Value Video must come to work on time.
- Employees who are late more than two times in a month will be put on probation.
- Employees who are late more than seven times in a month will be terminated.
- All employees must make an effort to be on time every day.

Main Idea: All employees must be on time.

Detail: More than 2 lates, employees will be put on probation.

Detail: More than seven lates, employees will be fired.

YOUR TURN

Read the paragraph from Tina's employee manual again. Then, using one of the note-taking strategies from this chapter, take notes based on your reading.

Chapter Six

R E V I E W

You have learned a lot already! Look at the checklist and check off what you learned. You can add some of your own ideas on the lines following the checklist.

When I take notes from textbooks I...

☐ look for the main idea and details. (Lesson 1)

☐ take notes on the most important information. (Lesson 1)

☐ use note pyramids to organize information. (Lesson 2)

☐ use word webs to organize information. (Lesson 3)

☐ use outlines to organize information. (Lesson 4)

☐ try different notes taking styles. (Lesson 5)

☐ use notes-taking styles that work for me. (Lesson 5)

☐ _____

☐ _____

☐ _____

☐ _____

☐ _____

☐ _____

☐ _____

☐ _____

☐ _____

☐ _____

Answer the following items about what you have learned in this chapter.

1. On a separate sheet of paper, use an outline to take notes on these paragraphs.

   > The deadliest tornado in the United States hit in 1925. Moving at 73 miles per hour, the storm ripped through 13 towns in Missouri, Illinois, and Indiana. In all, 695 people were killed, 2,000 injured, and 15,000 left homeless. The storm lasted over 3 hours and caused destruction over 164 square miles.
   >
   > Hurricane Andrew was the costliest storm in U.S. history. The hurricane hit southern Florida in August, 1992. Seventy-six people died in Hurricane Andrew. About 258,000 lost their homes. In all, the damage done by the storm amounted to $46.5 billion!
   >
   > The worst flood damage in the United States occurred in 1993. The flood affected nine states in the Midwest. It caused $12 billion in damage. At its peak, the flood covered an area twice the size of New Jersey.

2. On a separate sheet of paper, use a note pyramid to take notes on this paragraph.

   > Steven Spielberg is one of the most successful filmmakers. Seven of his movies are in the all-time top 10 movies. Together, Spielberg's movies have earned over $2.2 billion. Spielberg won his first "Best Director" Oscar for *Schindler's List*, a story about Jews in Nazi Germany.

3. On a separate sheet of paper, use a word web to take notes on this paragraph.

> Singer Michael Jackson gave the most successful concert series ever. He performed in London, England, for seven nights in 1988. Each night, the stadium, which held 72,000 people, was sold out. So a total of 504,000 fans paid to see the performances.

4. Turn to In the Workplace on page 84. Look over the employee handbook again. In small groups, discuss why taking notes at work is important. Finally, have one group member tell the class what your group thought.

Talk It Over

With a group of classmates, talk about what you have learned. Answer these questions:

▶ Where did Michael Jordan go to college?

▶ How much money did Michael Jordan make in 1997?

▶ Why is Michael Jordan considered one of the most successful atheletes ever?

chapter six

LEARNING STYLES CHECK-IN

Check off the ways you learn best. Then use the suggestions to help take and use notes from textbooks.

Word-smart learner

- Develop your notes into short paragraphs. Sum up the important ideas as clearly as possible.
- Speak up in class.

Sound-smart learner

- The next time you have a reading assignment in a textbook, use a tape recorder to take notes.

People-smart learner

- Compare notes with a friend. Check to see if you both have the same main points.
- Use your notes in a study group with three or four classmates.

Self-smart learner

- Work hard at developing your notes at home. Use a textbook to make sure you have all the important points covered.

Picture-smart learner

- Draw some of your notes. A picture can be worth a thousand words.
- Make up your own signs to use in notes.

Action-smart learner

- Act out events from your textbook with a group of classmates.

Number-smart learner

- Use charts and outlines to keep your notes in order.

Chapter
SEVEN

Memory Strategies

MATT'S MEMORY

Last year, Matt could never recall facts on tests. His grades were low. Matt blamed his bad memory.

Then Matt read an article about memory. It said memory was a set of skills. It claimed people could improve their memories. Matt tried some memory strategies.

Now Matt makes up pictures and rhymes to recall facts. These help a lot. He repeats information he needs over and over. He learned that reviewing is a big part of remembering.

Writing information helps Matt remember too. He makes charts when he studies. He uses flash cards to learn facts.

The strategies have helped Matt. His memory is better now. So are his grades!

What happened? Matt took the time to learn some memory strategies. Recall is a big part of studying. It is important for tests. The strategies in this chapter will help you remember more too.

What Do You Think?

▶ Why is it important to have a good memory?

▶ What do you do to remember things?

LESSON 1
Memory Aids

Key Term
memory aids tools to help you remember something

Have you ever heard this rhyme?

> *I* before *e*, except after *c*,
> Or when sounding like *a*, as in *neighbor* or *weigh*.

The rhyme is a memory aid. It helps you spell words with *ie* or *ei* in them. These words, such as *wield*, *freight*, and *receive*, are often spelled wrong.

Take a Look

Memory aids help you remember information. You can make up your own. Your teachers may also share some with you.

The word *HOMES* is a well-known memory aid. It helps you remember the names of the Great Lakes. They are Lake **H**uron, Lake **O**ntario, Lake **M**ichigan, Lake **E**rie, and Lake **S**uperior. Each letter in *HOMES* is the first letter of one of the lakes.

Mario used the memory rhyme below to help him check off the misspelled words:

> *I* before *e*, except after *c*,
> Or when sounding like *a*, as in *neighbor* or *weigh*.

__X__ reciept	____ pier	__X__ sliegh	____ conceited
____ belief	__X__ peice	____ thief	

Mental pictures are another memory aid. You can make up pictures to recall dates and names. Usually pictures that are unusual are easiest to remember.

Suppose, for example, you are studying the American Revolution. You have to remember that the Boston Tea Party happened in 1773. You might form a picture of a big cup of tea. On the cup, imagine the year 1773. That picture should help you remember.

You can use pictures to remember names too. For example, the Quartering Acts forced colonists to keep British soldiers in their houses. To remember that, think of a house cut into four quarters with an ax (Quartering Acts). In each quarter, imagine a British soldier and an angry colonist.

Try It Out

On a separate sheet of paper, draw a memory picture to remember one of these facts:

- At the Boston Massacre of 1770, five colonists were killed.

- The Declaration of Independence was signed in 1776.

- The Stamp Act taxed newspapers and other printed goods.

On Your Own

Sometimes you have to remember a series of people, places, and things. Making up a story can help. Include all the facts you need to know in one unusual or silly story. Tell the story to yourself a few times until you remember it.

1. On the lines below, list three or more facts you need to remember for social studies.

_____

_____

_____

2. Write a short, unusual story to help you remember these facts.

_____

_____

LESSON 2
Memory Skills

Memory is not just a place in your brain. It is more like a set of skills. No one is stuck with a bad memory. You can improve your memory by practicing memory skills.

Take a Look

Being more aware is one memory skill. The more you notice, the more you will remember. In a learning situation, try to notice everything. If you are reading, look closely at each page. Pay attention to the headings. Study the type and pictures. If you watch a videotape, look and listen for details. The more you see and hear, the more you will remember.

Repetition is another memory skill. Repeating a fact makes an impression. The more you repeat it, the more likely you are to recall it. It helps to say the fact aloud.

Be sure to make and use memory aids when you repeat information. You might form pictures to help you recall. Also, have faith in your memory. Tell yourself that your memory is getting better. Be confident that you can remember what you need to know!

Here is a list of 10 made-up words and their meanings. Study the list for 60 seconds. Repeat the words to yourself as often as you can. Then close your book. Write as many of the words and their meanings as you can remember on a separate sheet of paper.

plin	truck	*lendot*	apple
stant	computer	*rett*	pencil
imray	window	*slok*	desk
bloth	sunshine	*penda*	shirt
fasen	water	*drob*	friend

If you like, try the experiment again. This time repeat the words for two more minutes. How many can you remember this time?

Repeating information helps you remember it. You should repeat it often. This is called reviewing. Regular reviewing will help you succeed on tests.

When you review:

- Make sure the information is correct.
- Try to understand the information fully.
- Say the information aloud.
- Discuss the information with a study partner.

Practice being aware by making reviewing part of your regular study schedule. Before reading new material, review the old. When you make a study calendar, write in what you should review.

Try It Out

Look around your classroom. Imagine you are there for the very first time. Find three things that you never noticed before. Write them on the lines.

_____

_____

_____

On Your Own

Make a study calendar for this week. List any upcoming tests in the next week. For each test, also write a memory skill you can use.

 Remember, you already learned about study calendars on page 22.

MONDAY	TUESDAY	WEDNESDAY	THURSDAY	FRIDAY

LESSON 3
Write It Down

Key Term
timeline graphic that shows the order that things happened

Suppose a friend gave you an important phone number. You might say it a few times to remember it. If you wrote it down, though, you would feel more sure about not forgetting it.

The same is true when studying. You are more likely to remember information when you write it down.

Take a Look

Often you need to recall dates and events on tests. Writing them down while you study will help. You can write dates and events on a **timeline**. A timeline shows the order that things happened. It also shows how much time passed between events.

Look at the timeline below. Timelines have a lot of information to offer.

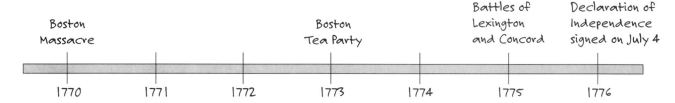

| Boston Massacre | | | Boston Tea Party | | Battles of Lexington and Concord | Declaration of Independence signed on July 4 |

1770   1771   1772   1773   1774   1775   1776

Try It Out

Teri recalls the following events and dates from her history class. To fix them in her memory, she decides to list them on a timeline.

Declaration of Independence signed July 4, 1776

1773–Boston Tea Party–colonists protest tea tax by throwing tea into ocean

Battles of Lexington and Concord–1775–first fighting of Revolution

Boston Massacre of 1770–Feelings between people of Boston and British soldiers get worse

Complete the timeline. Write the dates and events in order.

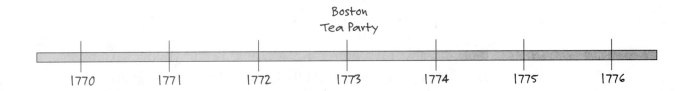

Boston
Tea Party

|1770 |1771 |1772 |1773 |1774 |1775 |1776

Writing a short summary is another way to remember information. A summary gives the most important information on a topic. It gives the main ideas but not the details. Usually that is all you will need to know for a test.

On Your Own

Read this passage from a social studies textbook. Try to remember what you read.

SOCIAL STUDIES

New Taxes In 1767, Britain passed the Townshend Acts. These acts taxed products that the colonists got from Britain. Cloth, paper, paint, and glass were taxed. People in Boston strongly opposed the new taxes.

British officials went to Boston to collect the taxes. These tax collectors had great power. They could search the homes and businesses of colonists for goods. These searches took place without warning. Tax collectors did not need to get permission from a judge.

Now write one or two sentences to sum up the passage from what you remember.

_____

_____

_____

LESSON 4
Using Flash Cards

You probably used flash cards when you were younger. You may have learned new words on flash cards. Maybe you memorized math facts with them.

Take a Look

You can still use flash cards to memorize information. All you need is a pack of 3 x 5 index cards. There is not much room on each card. So, on the front of a card, list just one name, event, or idea. On the back, write what it is and why it is important.

To use the cards, look at the front. See what you can recall about the topic. Then turn the card over. Check whether you are right.

Here is the front of a flash card that Jeri made for social studies:

Declaration of Independence

Here is the back of the same card.

written by Thomas Jefferson with help from Benjamin Franklin and John Adams

adopted on July 4, 1776 (Independence Day)

listed ways the British king was unfair

claimed that "all men are created equal"

Flash cards make reviewing easy. Take them with you wherever you go. When you are on a bus, take out your cards. If you have a break at a job, use your cards. It is easy to turn wasted time into study time. Flash cards let you review regularly. That, of course, is the key to remembering information.

Try It Out

Use this information to make a flash card. Use the front and the back of the flash card shown below.

Battles of Lexington and Concord—April 19, 1775. 1st battles of Revol. British tried to capture American guns. Paul Revere warned minutemen. Fighting broke out. Br. had heavy losses.

Front

Battles of Lexington and Concord

Back

On Your Own

Use index cards to make a set of flash cards. Choose one subject in which you have a test coming up. Look over your notes and textbook to see what you need to review. Use the lines below to list some of the topics you will write on the cards.

_____

_____

_____

_____

_____

A résumé sums up your education and work experience. Having a résumé will help you get a job. A résumé usually includes important information.

Look at the résumé José created for himself.

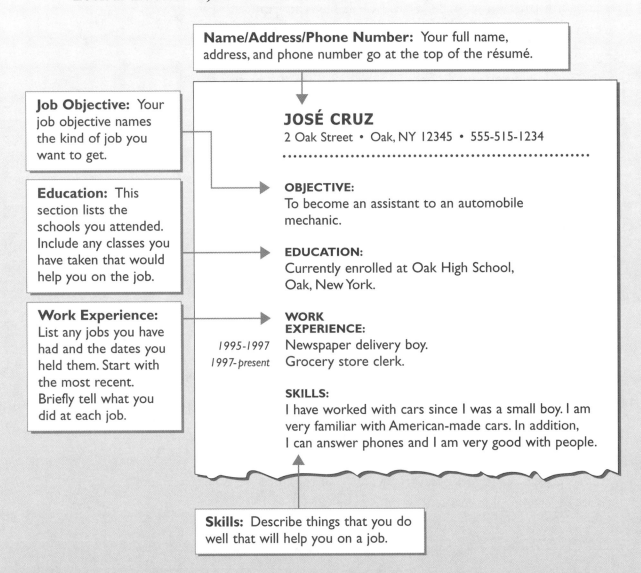

Name/Address/Phone Number: Your full name, address, and phone number go at the top of the résumé.

Job Objective: Your job objective names the kind of job you want to get.

Education: This section lists the schools you attended. Include any classes you have taken that would help you on the job.

Work Experience: List any jobs you have had and the dates you held them. Start with the most recent. Briefly tell what you did at each job.

JOSÉ CRUZ
2 Oak Street • Oak, NY 12345 • 555-515-1234

OBJECTIVE:
To become an assistant to an automobile mechanic.

EDUCATION:
Currently enrolled at Oak High School, Oak, New York.

WORK EXPERIENCE:
1995-1997 Newspaper delivery boy.
1997-present Grocery store clerk.

SKILLS:
I have worked with cars since I was a small boy. I am very familiar with American-made cars. In addition, I can answer phones and I am very good with people.

Skills: Describe things that you do well that will help you on a job.

YOUR TURN

Ask your teacher to provide you with a blank résumé form to fill out. Choose a job you might be interested in and fill out your own résumé.

Chapter Seven

REVIEW

You have learned a lot already! Look at the checklist and check off what you learned. You can add some of your own ideas on the lines following the checklist.

In order to remember better, I:

☐ try to make up memory aids. (Lesson 1)

☐ form unusual images and stories that help me remember certain facts. (Lesson 1)

☐ pay close attention to details when I read. (Lesson 2)

☐ repeat key facts in my mind. (Lesson 2)

☐ review information regularly when I study. (Lesson 2)

☐ write down information I need to remember. (Lesson 3)

☐ use timelines to write down information. (Lesson 3)

☐ create flash cards for the subjects I study. (Lesson 4)

☐ place a topic on one side of the flash card and information about it on the other. (Lesson 4)

☐ use my flash cards to study when I have spare time. (Lesson 4)

☐ _____

☐ _____

☐ _____

CHAPTER SEVEN PRACTICE

Answer the following items about what you have learned in this chapter.

1. List four memory aids that will help you remember more when studying.

   a. _____

   b. _____

   c. _____

   d. _____

2. The American Civil War took place between 1861 and 1865. In the war, states in the North fought against states in the South. Think of a memory picture to remember these dates. Describe your image on the following lines.

   _____

   _____

   _____

   _____

3. Seti has to remember the colors of the spectrum in the right order. The colors are red, orange, yellow, green, blue, indigo, and violet. As a memory aid, Seti uses the name ROY G. BIV. Each letter in that name is the first letter of a color. That name also gives the colors in their correct order.

   On the following lines, write the colors of the spectrum. Write them in their correct order, beginning with red.

   _____

   _____

   _____

   _____

4. Place this information on the flash card below.

The Townshend Acts taxed goods shipped from Britain to the colonies. The 1767 acts put taxes on paper, glass, paint, and cloth.

Front

Back

5. Place these dates and events on the timeline.

- The first women's college opens in 1837.

- The Seneca Falls Convention of 1848 starts the women's rights movement.

- In 1821, the first high school for women opens.

1820   1830   1840   1850

Talk It Over

With a group of classmates, talk about what you have learned. Answer these questions:

▶ What were the first two battles of the American Revolution?

▶ How many colonists were killed at the Boston Massacre?

LEARNING STYLES CHECK-IN

Check off the ways you learn best. Then use the suggestions to help yourself remember information.

Word-smart learner

- Make up acronyms. Each letter in an acronym stands for the first letter of a word you have to remember.

Sound-smart learner

- Make up rhymes and jingles to recall facts. Do not worry if they are silly. You do not have to share them.

- Recite, recite, recite! When you say information aloud, your mind organizes it in a way you can use.

People-smart learner

- Use flash cards with a friend. Your friend shows you the front of the card. You tell your friend what should be on the back.

- Schedule study groups with a few classmates.

Self-smart learner

- Think hard about what you have to remember. Tell yourself it is important.

- Be positive! Remind yourself that you can improve your memory.

Picture-smart learner

- Form strong mental pictures of things to remember. Make the picture as big and as bright as it needs to be.

Action-smart learner

- Be alert and relaxed when you study. You will remember more.

Number-smart learner

- Keep track of how many times you have to review a fact to remember it.

Chapter
EIGHT

Test Taking

MARCO AND RENEE

Marco and Renee have to take a test next Friday. Notice how different their attitudes are.

Marco tells himself, "I hate tests! I never do well!" Marco studies during the week, but it is hard to focus. On the day of the test, he is tired and confused. When he gets his test back, Marco's grade is low. He throws the test paper away without looking at his mistakes. "The teacher is too hard!" he decides.

Renee sees the test as a challenge. Her goal is to do better on this test than the last one. She gives herself enough time to review everything. She arrives in class in plenty of time. Renee stays relaxed during the test. She reads the questions carefully.

Renee does better on this test than on the last one. She reads over the test carefully to check what she did wrong. She does not want to make the same mistakes next time!

What happened? Renee has learned some important test-taking skills. Marco has not. By practicing the skills in this chapter, you can improve your grades too.

What Do You Think?

▶   What can you do *not* to be nervous about tests?

▶   What common mistakes do students make on tests?

LESSON 1
Taming Test Fears

No one looks forward to tests. However, you do not have to be afraid of them. Fearing tests is not good for you. When you are afraid, your body tenses up. Sometimes you cannot think clearly. It is easy to make silly mistakes on tests when you are afraid.

Take a Look

Are you afraid of tests? Check the statements that describe you.

_____ I walk into the test knowing I will not do well.

_____ I never really feel ready for a test.

_____ During the test, my hands sweat, and it is hard to breathe.

_____ I get more and more tense when I do not know answers.

_____ I sometimes forget to bring pens and pencils for a test.

_____ I think the other students are doing better than I am.

Did you check more than one? Then chances are you have test-taking fears. Luckily, there are ways to tame those fears. Here are some tips to try:

> • Be prepared. Make sure you have reviewed everything that will be on the test.
>
> • Get to the test on time and relax.
>
> • Read over the whole test before you start. Find the easy parts and the hard parts. Decide how much time to spend on each.
>
> • Do an easy part first. That might get you over your fear.
>
> • If you start to feel fear, close your eyes and take a deep breath.
>
> • Do not pay attention to anyone else.
>
> • Keep a positive attitude. Tell yourself that you will do well.
>
> • Read direction lines carefully.

Try It Out

Read how Sheila took her social science test. On the lines below, write three things that Sheila probably did wrong.

> Sheila got to her test a little late. Everyone else had begun. She started right away on the first part, the true or false questions. It was worth 20 points. Sheila was not really sure of the answers, so she began to tense up. She decided to go on to the multiple-choice questions. She did a few. Then she looked down and saw the essay question. It was worth 60 points. Usually she did well on essays. Should she start it? Or should she go back and finish the other questions? Time was running out! Sheila groaned. She was sure she was going to fail!

1. _____

2. _____

3. _____

Making a quick test clock would have helped Sheila. A test clock shows what is on a test. It shows how much each section of a test is worth. Sheila's test clock might have looked like this.

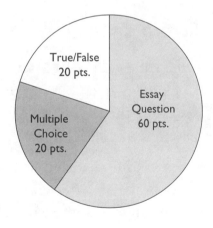

True/False 20 pts.

Essay Question 60 pts.

Multiple Choice 20 pts.

The clock shows that Sheila should have spent at least half her time on the essay.

On Your Own

On a separate sheet of paper, write a few sentences that describe how you prepare for a test. Now that you have read this lesson, also include anything you would add to your preparation. Then read what you have written to a partner. Compare what your partner has written to what you have written.

LESSON 2
Taking Objective Tests

You will often take objective tests. Each question on an objective test has one right answer. True or false questions, for example, are on objective tests. So are multiple-choice questions. Fill-in-the-blank and matching questions are also objective.

Here are some tips for taking objective tests:

- Read the directions carefully. Be sure you know where and how to mark your answers.

- Answer the easy questions first. Then go back to the harder ones and answer them.

- Answer every question. If you are not sure, guess at the answer.

- Go back and check your answers. Do not change an answer unless you are sure you made a mistake.

Take a Look

TRUE OR FALSE QUESTIONS

True or false questions test how well you recognize information. Reviewing the facts in your notes will help you answer these questions. If you are not sure of an answer, remember:

- Few broad statements are true. Be on the lookout for qualifying words like *all*, *always*, *no*, and *never* in true or false questions. Statements with these words are often false. If you can think of one exception to the statement, it is false.

- Some qualifying words signal a true statement. These words are *often*, *many*, *some*, *most*, and *sometimes*. If you can think of one example of the statement, it is true.

MULTIPLE-CHOICE QUESTIONS

Here are some tips to help you on multiple-choice questions:

- Think what the answer might be before reading the choices. If your answer is one of the choices, it is probably right.

- If the questions are based on a reading passage, read the questions first. Then you will know what to look for as you read.

- Eliminate as many wrong answers as you can. Then you are more likely to guess the right answer.

- "All of the above" is often correct. That is especially true if you are pretty sure that two of the answer choices are correct.

Try It Out

Read these true or false questions. Circle the qualifying word in each.

1. All songbirds in the United States today are in danger of dying out.

2. Since the 1970s, some wild mammal populations have increased.

3. No one opposes letting wolves loose in Yellowstone National Park.

On Your Own

Work with a friend. Find objective questions from old tests you have taken. Go over your answers. What types of mistakes did you make? How could you have done better on these questions? Make a list of tips for taking objective tests.

_____

_____

_____

_____

LESSON 3
Taking Subjective Tests

Key Term

command words words that suggest how you should
answer a question

Subjective tests have essay questions. There is no one correct
answer to an essay question. Your teacher expects to find certain
information in your answers though.

Take a Look

Here are some tips for answering essay questions:

- Be sure you understand what the question is asking.

- Jot down the facts and ideas that should be in the answer.

- In the opening sentences or paragraph, sum up the key points.

- Write the essay, using your notes.

Often you can use the essay question itself in your opening
sentence. Shironda found this essay question on her test.

> Describe the main reason why the mountain lion population
> increased in the United States after 1970.

Shironda reworded the question this way to open her essay:

> After 1970, the mountain lion population in the United
> States increased mainly due to the limits placed on
> hunting by western lawmakers.

In the rest of her answer, Shironda described her two points.

Many essay questions have **command words**. The command word
suggests how to answer the question.

Essay Command Word	How to Answer It
compare	Show how things are alike.
contrast	Show how things are different.
explain	Give causes or reasons.
define	Tell what it means.
describe	Give facts and details.

Try It Out

Circle the command word in the question. How would you answer the question?

Earth's largest mammals, the elephant and the whale, both face problems in trying to survive. Contrast the problems that these two mammals face.

On Your Own

Daryl read this essay question on his science test:

> Define the terms *extinct* and *endangered*, when used to describe wildlife. Give examples of animals in each category.

Daryl jotted down these notes:

> (1) extinct: all members dead; species will not return; passenger pigeons, dodo birds.
> (2) endangered: population has declined; species could die out; Florida panthers, manatees.

Use Daryl's notes to write an answer to the essay question on a separate sheet of paper.

LESSON 4
Taking Standardized Tests

Most tests are made up by your teachers. They test what you have learned in class recently. Standardized tests are different. Students all over the state or country take them. They test what you have learned during all your years in school. They often test English and math skills. These tests have lots of questions. They take a long time.

Take a Look

GENERAL TIPS

Some people say you cannot study for standardized tests. Actually, there are ways to prepare for them. For one thing, you can find out ahead of time what tests you will take. You can also practice on sample tests. These will show you what to expect.

You may not be able to study for a standardized test. Still, there are ways to improve your score. Here are some tips to help you on standardized tests:

- Look over the whole test first. Make a test clock.

- Start at the beginning. The questions on these tests often go from easy to hard.

- Find out if you lose points for wrong answers. If so, do not guess. Go back to questions you are not sure of later if there is time.

- Mark the answer sheet correctly and neatly. If you miss a line on the answer sheet, every answer will be wrong!

ANALOGIES

Standardized tests use analogies to test your thinking. Analogies show relationships between pairs of words. An example of an analogy is given below. You read it, "Flower is to garden as tree is to _____?"

---

flower: garden::tree: _____
a. bark   b. branch   c. forest   d. soil

To solve an analogy, figure out how the first two words are related. How is flower related to a garden? A flower is part of a garden. So the relationship is part to whole. Next ask, "With which answer choice does a tree have a part-whole relationship? A tree is part of a forest. So the answer is *c*.

Try It Out

Here are the answers for questions 1–6 of a standardized test.

1. C **2.** D **3.** A **4.** A **5.** B **6.** B

Mark the answers on the sample answer sheet below. Be sure to fill in the circles completely.

---

1. Ⓐ Ⓑ Ⓒ Ⓓ Ⓔ   **4.** Ⓐ Ⓑ Ⓒ Ⓓ Ⓔ

2. Ⓐ Ⓑ Ⓒ Ⓓ Ⓔ   **5.** Ⓐ Ⓑ Ⓒ Ⓓ Ⓔ

3. Ⓐ Ⓑ Ⓒ Ⓓ Ⓔ   **6.** Ⓐ Ⓑ Ⓒ Ⓓ Ⓔ

On Your Own

Solve these analogies.

1. dog:puppy::flower: _____
   a. bud   **b.** leaf   **c.** garden   **d.** colors

2. apple:seed::chicken: _____
   a. egg   **b.** meat   **c.** feather   **d.** farm

3. belt:buckle::suitcase: _____
   a. leather   **b.** clothes   **c.** lock   **d.** trunk

Filling out answers correctly is very important on standardized tests. It is also an important skill when you fill out official documents and forms.

Many official agencies process hundreds of forms in a day. It is very important that the information on the forms be neat, correct, and easy to read.

Melissa needs to fill out this form to replace her Social Security card. She has to be careful not to make a mistake when she fills in her name, address, and Social Security number. Melissa writes neatly so that it is easy to read.

SOCIAL SECURITY ADMINISTRATION
Application for a Social Security Card

1	NAME To Be Shown on Card	▶ Melissa	Deborah	Smith
		FIRST	FULL MIDDLE NAME	LAST
	FULL NAME AT BIRTH IF OTHER THAN ABOVE	FIRST	FULL MIDDLE NAME	LAST
	OTHER NAMES USED			
2	MAILING ADDRESS Do Not Abbreviate	▶ 123	Pine	Street
		STREET ADDRESS, APT. NO., PO BOX, RURAL ROUTE NO.		
		Palm	Florida	01234
		CITY	STATE	ZIP CODE

3	DATE OF BIRTH	11/6/1983	4	PLACE OF BIRTH	Palm	Florida
		MONTH DAY YEAR			CITY	STATE OR FOREIGN COUNTRY

5	YOUR SIGNATURE	*Melissa D. Smith*	7/7/1999
			DATE

YOUR TURN

Ask your teacher for a blank Social Security form. Fill in the information you would need to replace your Social Security card.

Chapter Eight

REVIEW

You have learned a lot already! Look at the checklist and check off what you have learned.

Whenever I take tests, I:

☐ skim the whole test before I start. (Lesson 1)

☐ read the directions carefully. (Lesson 1)

When I take objective tests, I:

☐ answer the easy questions and then go back and do harder ones. (Lesson 2)

☐ look for qualifying words, such as *always, never,* and *most* in true or false questions. (Lesson 2)

☐ eliminate wrong choices before guessing at multiple choice questions. (Lesson 2)

When I take subjective tests, I:

☐ note the points I will make in my answer before beginning to write. (Lesson 3)

☐ use the essay question itself to word my opening sentence. (Lesson 3)

☐ look for command words, such as *compare* or *explain,* in the question to decide how to answer it. (Lesson 3)

When I take standardized tests, I:

☐ get familiar with the test format ahead of time. (Lesson 4)

☐ take care to fill out the answer sheet correctly. (Lesson 4)

CHAPTER EIGHT PRACTICE

Answer the following items about what you have learned in Chapter 8.

1. List three ways you can tame test fears.

   _____

   _____

   _____

2. Name one important fact to remember about true or false questions.

   _____

   _____

3. Name one important fact to remember about multiple-choice questions.

   _____

   _____

4. What do the command words below mean?

   Compare: _____

   Contrast: _____

   Explain: _____

   Define: _____

   Describe: _____

5. Fill in the answer sheet below with the following answers:
1. A; 2. C; 3. B; 4. E; 5. A; 6. D. Make sure you fill in
the answers neatly.

1. Ⓐ Ⓑ Ⓒ Ⓓ Ⓔ		**4.** Ⓐ Ⓑ Ⓒ Ⓓ Ⓔ
2. Ⓐ Ⓑ Ⓒ Ⓓ Ⓔ		**5.** Ⓐ Ⓑ Ⓒ Ⓓ Ⓔ
3. Ⓐ Ⓑ Ⓒ Ⓓ Ⓔ		**6.** Ⓐ Ⓑ Ⓒ Ⓓ Ⓔ

6. Why is it important to fill in an answer sheet correctly?

_____

_____

_____

Talk It Over

With a group of classmates, talk about what you have learned.
Answer these questions:

▶ What is the difference between an endangered species and
an extinct species?

▶ Why did the mountain lion population increase in the
United States after 1970?

LEARNING STYLES CHECK-IN

Check off the ways you learn. Then use the suggestions when taking tests.

Word-smart learner

- Study by writing your own test questions. Chances are you will cover the same points as your teacher.

Sound-smart learner

- Make a tape to motivate yourself. Tape all the reasons you will do well on tests. Play the tape before each test.

People-smart learner

- Talk to your teacher before a test. Make sure you know what the test will cover.
- Form a test study group with some friends.

Self-smart learner

- Review all the questions in your textbook before a test. Chances are the teacher will cover the same points.

Picture-smart learner

- Try the power of positive thinking! Form a picture of yourself doing well on a test.

Action-smart learner

- Relax your body before a test. Take a few deep breaths.
- Keep a high-energy snack handy just in case.

Number-smart learner

- Make a list of the topics likely to be on a test. Estimate how important each is. Use that to decide how much time to spend studying each topic.
- Check your last few tests. Find your averages in objective and subjective parts. Use that information to plan your study time.

part **one** ▤ **wrap-up**

In Part 1, you learned about strategies to help you make the most out of your study time. Now you can fill in this action plan with all of the things you learned.

The following chart lists the topics of each chapter. Fill in the chart with the most important things you learned. Review this chart the next time you sit down to study.

Action Plan

Chapter 1 through Chapter 8	
Chapter 1 Setting Goals for Yourself	**Chapter 5** Note Taking in Class
Chapter 2 Organizing Yourself	**Chapter 6** Note Taking From Textbooks
Chapter 3 Using Your Resources	**Chapter 7** Memory Strategies
Chapter 4 Understanding What You Read	**Chapter 8** Test Taking

What Do You Think?

Which of the strategies you learned will help you the most?

_____

_____

part **two**

CONTENT-AREA STUDY SKILLS

As a student, you have studied for your language arts, math, social science, and science classes. You need to study each content area a little differently. This part of the book will teach you skills and strategies to help you study these content areas.

Here is what you will learn in Part 2:

CHAPTER 9
Language Arts

CHAPTER 10
Mathematics

CHAPTER 11
Social Science

CHAPTER 12
Science

Brainstorm!

In Part 2, you will learn about taking notes in language arts, math, social science, and science. In small groups, discuss note taking in each of the content areas. How is taking notes different? How is taking notes the same? Make a list and share your list with the class.

Chapter
NINE

Language Arts

KAMAL CANNOT CONNECT

Kamal has to read a short story for English. He opens his book to the page. Kamal has no idea what the story is about. He does not know where or when it takes place.

The first few paragraphs have some hard words. Kamal does not know what they mean. So he skips them. He hopes they will not matter too much.

Midway through the story, Kamal is having trouble. He cannot connect with the story. He is having a hard time keeping track of the characters. His mind wanders. He loses his place. He is not sure whether he has read some sections or not.

There are questions at the end of the story. Kamal has to answer them. He does not think he will be able to answer them. "Why do we have to read this story anyway?" he wonders.

What happened? Kamal tried to read the story. He couldn't connect with it though. Kamal needs to get more involved in the reading process. He needs to become a more active reader. In this chapter, we will look at some ways to connect with the stories you read in English class.

What Do You Think?

► What advice would you give Kamal?

► What do you do when you have trouble connecting with a story?

LESSON 1
How to Use Resources

Tools that help you study are called resources. The dictionary and thesaurus are a big help in English class.

Take a Look

DICTIONARY

 You learned about study resources in Chapter 3.

Kamal is reading a Greek myth in English class. It is called "Atalanta's Race." Here is the first paragraph:

Atalanta's Race

Atalanta was the most beautiful woman in ancient Greece. She was also the fastest runner. Many men wanted to marry her. She refused to marry though. To get rid of her **suitors**, she announced a strange plan. "I will only marry the man who can beat me in a race!" she said. "But anyone who races me and loses will die!"

Kamal is not sure of the meaning of the word *suitors*. So he looks it up in a dictionary. Here is the entry he finds.

Study these parts of the dictionary entry:

Pronunciation: This respelling shows how to say the word. An accent (´) or capital letters show which syllable is louder.

Part of Speech: The *n* shows the word is a noun. A *v* is used for a verb. *Adj* and *adv* show adjectives and adverbs.

Word History: This is how the word came into English. *Suitor* came from a Latin word meaning "follower."

Entry word: The entry word shows the spelling. It also shows how the word can be divided.

suit or \ˈsu-tər\ *n.* [L *secutor* follower. fr. *sequi* to follow]
1. one who asks for something 2. one who sues in a court of law 3. one who courts a woman or seeks to marry her.

Meanings. Many words have more than one meaning. Three meanings are given for *suitor*.

Kamal wants to know what *suitors* means. To find out, he looks at the three meanings in the entry:

MEANING 1: one who asks for something
MEANING 2: one who sues in a court of law
MEANING 3: one who courts a woman or seeks to marry her

Kamal decides on Meaning 3. This meaning shows how *suitors* is used in the story.

THESAURUS

Sometimes you may use the same word too often. A thesaurus can help. Use a thesaurus to find substitute words.

Kamal has finished reading "Atalanta's Race." Now he is writing a response to the myth.

Many men in ancient Greece loved Atalanta. She didn't love any of them though. Hippomenes also loved Atalanta. She didn't love him at first either.

Kamal sees that he uses the word love too often. So he looks up *love* in a thesaurus. He finds these synonyms.

love (luv) *n.* adore, care for, fall for, lose one's heart to, idolize, prize, treasure, worship

Kamal rewrites the paragraph. He substitutes synonyms for *love*. He tries to find just the right synonyms.

Many men in ancient Greece idolized Atalanta. She didn't care for any of them though. Hippomenes also lost his heart to Atalanta. She didn't fall for him at first either.

You can also use a thesaurus if your writing seems lifeless. You may be using vague words. Vague words do not show a clear picture. A thesaurus is a good place to find more precise words.

Vague	Precise
She gave me a *nice look*.	She gave me a *sunny smile*.
He *went slowly* down the way.	He *lumbered* down the way.
I read a *good book*.	I read a *gripping mystery*.

Try It Out

USING A DICTIONARY

Kamal continues to read the myth. Here is the next paragraph:

> The suitors were willing to **hazard** all for Atalanta. So a race was arranged. Handsome young Hippomenes was the judge. As he watched the runners, he was struck by Atalanta's beauty. She moved like the wind. Speed fanned her beauty to a glow. Love for Atalanta seized his heart.

Kamal wonders about the word *hazard*. So he looks it up in the dictionary. Here are the entries he finds.

> ¹**hazard**   (ˈhaz ərd) *n.* [French *hasard,* fr. Arabic *az-zahr* dice] 1. a game of chance played with two dice 2. a source of danger 3. a risk or chance.
> ²**haz ard**   *v.* to risk or take a chance.

Answer these questions about the entry words.

1. Which syllable of *hazard* is said louder—the first or the second?

2. How many meanings are given for the noun *hazard*? _____

3. The word *hazard* is used as a verb in the myth. So the meaning

   of *hazard* in the myth is: _____

USING A THESAURUS

Kamal wrote these sentences about "Atalanta's Race." Later, he underlined some vague words and looked them up in a thesaurus.

Here are some synonyms that Kamal found. Circle a more precise synonym for each vague word. Choose words that work well in the sentences.

> In my view, Atalanta was <u>bad</u> to the <u>men</u>. She <u>asked</u> them to compete in an event that they would surely lose.

1. **bad:** unfair, cruel, naughty, base, ill
2. **men:** fellows, friends, partners, suitors, neighbors
3. **asked:** invited, called, demanded, challenged

On Your Own

Here is the third paragraph of the myth. Look up the underlined words in a dictionary. Write the meaning of the word as it is used in the sentence.

> Alas, the young men were no match for Atalanta. They grew <u>faint</u>. She flew ahead. When Atalanta reached the goal, they <u>lagged</u> far behind. Sadly, they were led away and <u>condemned</u>.

1. faint _____

2. lagged _____

3. condemned _____

Find out how to use the thesaurus on a computer. Then open a file for a paper you have written. Find three words that you think are vague. Use the computer thesaurus to replace them. Note the words and why you changed them on the lines below. If you do not have any files on a computer, use a paper and a regular thesaurus.

Original Word	New Word	Why I Changed It
_____	_____	_____
_____	_____	_____
_____	_____	_____

LESSON 2
Active Reading

Do you like to watch previews for new movies? Previews give you a quick look at a film. They show you what to expect.

Take a Look

You can also preview when you read. Previewing gives you a quick look at a story or book. It lets you know what to expect.

How do you preview a story? First, think about the title. Look at the illustrations. Skim through the text to get an idea of what it is all about.

Predicting is part of previewing. Predicting is guessing what will happen. As you preview a story, predict what you think might happen. Base your prediction on what you already know.

Predicting gets you into the story. You will want to read on to see if your predictions are correct.

Setting a purpose for reading can help you focus on a book. To set a purpose for reading, ask yourself a question. Your question should be about the story. It should be a question the story is likely to answer.

As you read, keep your mind on your question. Try to answer it. Also think about whether your predictions come true.

Atalanta's Race

Atalanta was the most beautiful woman in ancient Greece. She was also the fastest runner. Many men wanted to marry her. She refused to marry though. To get rid of her suitors, she announced a strange plan. "I will only marry the man who can beat me in a race!" she said. "But anyone who races me and loses will die!"

The suitors were willing to hazard all for Atalanta. So a race was arranged. Handsome young Hippomenes was the judge.

As he watched the runners, he was struck by Atalanta's beauty. She moved like the wind. Speed fanned her beauty to a glow. Love for Atalanta seized his heart.

Alas, the young men were no match for Atalanta. They grew faint. She flew ahead. When Atalanta reached the goal, they lagged far behind. Sadly, they were led away and condemned.

Suddenly, Hippomenes, the judge, stood up. What he said surprised everyone. "I wish to try my fortune in a race with Atalanta too!"

After reading this passage, Tara predicted what she thought would happen. Then she asked a question about the story to help her set a purpose for her reading

Prediction: Hippomenes will win the race against Atalanta.

Purpose Question: How will Hippomenes win the race even though Atalanta is faster?

Tara's previewing will help her as she continues reading. She has predicted what she thinks will happen. She has also asked a question that she wants to know the answer to.

Try It Out

Before you read the next section from "Atalanta's Race" on the next page, set a purpose for reading. Think about what you already know about the story. Then ask yourself a question about what you want to know. Write your prediction and your question on the following lines.

_____

_____

_____

_____

Atalanta looked at Hippomenes sadly. He was younger and more handsome than the others. She did not want him to die. But her friends urged her to get ready. So with a heavy heart she agreed to another race.

Meanwhile, Hippomenes called on Venus, the Goddess of Love. "Let me be swift to win the race," he said. "Just as I have been swift to fall in love with Atalanta."

Venus was not far off. She heard Hippomenes. In fact, she had already moved his heart to love Atalanta. Now she came invisibly to his side. Into his hand, she slipped three golden apples. She also whispered advice in his ear.

The signal was given. Atalanta and Hippomenes were off! They ran like the wind. They ran so fast, they did not leave footprints. The race was long though. After a while, Hippomenes fell behind.

At that moment, Hippomenes tossed ahead the first apple. The golden fruit caught Atalanta's eye. Full of wonder, she stopped to pick it up. Hippomenes ran on and passed Atalanta.

On Your Own

Look back at the prediction Tara made in Take a Look. Was it correct? _____

Also reread your question from Try It Out. Can you answer it yet?

_____

Think about the prediction you made. You may need to make new ones. Base them on what you have read so far. Also think about your question. You may need to update it too.

Before reading the end of the story, write one more prediction on the lines on the next page. Also, update or rewrite your question.

Prediction: _____

_____

Question: _____

_____

> Soon Atalanta caught up. So Hippomenes threw another apple. Atalanta could not pass it by. She stopped and picked it up. Again, she fell behind.
>
> Once again, Atalanta caught up. Now the finish line was near. The two ran side by side.
>
> Hippomenes tossed the last apple. Atalanta would have left it alone. However, Venus made her want this apple most of all. So Atalanta stopped again. As she did, Hippomenes won the race.
>
> That is how Atalanta married Hippomenes. All went well too. For Venus filled Atalanta's heart with love for her husband.

Before finishing the story, I predicted that _____

_____

_____

My prediction (was/was not) correct because _____

_____

My purpose question was _____

_____

_____

The answer to this question is _____

_____

_____

LESSON 3
Note Taking in Language Arts

Key Term
Story map a graphic way to take notes about a story

When you travel to a new place, a map is a big help. With a map, you will not get lost or confused.

Take a Look

When you read a story, a **story map** can help you take notes. A story map notes the important parts of a story.

CHARACTERS A story map begins with the main characters. Those are the people in the story. Your notes should name each main character. You should also tell a little bit about them.

SETTING The story map also notes the setting. The setting is where and when the story takes place.

PROBLEM After the setting, a story map tells the problem. The problem is a difficulty the characters face.

EVENTS A story map should also list the events of the plot. The plot of a story is what happens. Only note the important plot events. Describe them in your own words. These events should sum up the story.

THEME Most stories have a message too. Sometimes it is called the theme. The theme is a message you get from reading the story.

SOLUTION Story characters usually solve their problem. The ending of a story shows the solution. A story map should show a solution too. At the end of a story map, list the solution. Tell how the characters solve their problem.

Atalanta's Race

Atalanta was the most beautiful woman in ancient Greece. She was also the fastest runner. Many men wanted to marry her. She refused to marry though. To get rid of her suitors, she announced a strange plan. "I will only marry the man who can beat me in a race!" she said. "But anyone who races me and loses, will die!"

The suitors were willing to hazard all for Atalanta. So a race was arranged. Handsome young Hippomenes was the judge. As he watched the runners, he was struck by Atalanta's beauty. She moved like the wind. Speed fanned her beauty to a glow. Love for Atalanta seized his heart.

Alas, the young men were no match for Atalanta. They grew faint. She flew ahead. When Atalanta reached the goal, they lagged far behind. Sadly, they were led away and condemned.

Suddenly, Hippomenes, the judge, stood up. What he said surprised everyone. "I wish to try my fortune in a race with Atalanta too!"

A STORY MAP FOR "ATALANTA'S RACE"

CHARACTERS	SETTING	PROBLEMS
Atalanta, a beautiful woman and a very fast runner. Hippomenes, a young man who falls in love with Atalanta	a foot race in ancient Greece	Hippomenes wants to marry Atalanta, but to do so he must beat her in a race. If he loses, he will die.

EVENT 1: Atalanta got rid of all her suitors by beating them in a race.

EVENT 2: Hippomenes decided he wanted to race Atalanta too.

EVENT 3: Atalanta sadly agreed to the race.

THEME Atalanta has many suitors.

SOLUTION Atalanta announces that she will only marry a man that can beat her in a race.

Try It Out

Here is the next part of "Atalanta's Race." After you read it, look at the story map on the next page. Some parts have been done for you. Fill in the rest of the story map.

Atalanta looked at Hippomenes sadly. He was younger and more handsome than the others. She did not want him to die. But her friends urged her to rest and get ready. So with a heavy heart she agreed to another race.

Meanwhile Hippomenes called on Venus, the Goddess of Love. "Let me be swift to win the race," he said. "Just as I have been swift to fall in love with Atalanta."

Venus was not far off. She heard Hippomenes. In fact, she had already moved his heart to love Atalanta. Now she came invisibly to his side. Into his hand, she slipped three golden apples. She also whispered advice in his ear.

The signal was given. Atalanta and Hippomenes were off! They ran like the wind. They ran so fast, they did not leave footprints. The race was long though. After a while, Hippomenes fell behind.

At that moment, Hippomenes tossed ahead the first apple. The golden fruit caught Atalanta's eye. Full of wonder, she stopped to pick it up. Hippomenes ran on and passed Atalanta.

Soon Atalanta caught up. So Hippomenes threw another apple. Atalanta could not pass it by. She stopped and picked it up. Again, she fell behind.

Once again, Atalanta caught up. Now the finish line was near. The two ran side by side.

A STORY MAP FOR "ATALANTA'S RACE"

CHARACTERS	SETTING	PROBLEMS
Atalanta, a beautiful woman and a very fast runner. Hippomenes, a young man who falls in love with Atalanta		

EVENT 1: Hippomenes calls on Venus, the Goddess of Love

EVENT 2:

EVENT 3:

THEME

SOLUTION

On Your Own

Read the last paragraphs of "Atalanta's Race." After you read, write the story solution and the story theme on a separate sheet of paper.

> Hippomenes tossed the last apple. Atalanta would have left it alone. However, Venus made her want this apple most of all. So Atalanta stopped again. As she did, Hippomenes won the race.
>
> That is how Atalanta married Hippomenes. All went well too. For Venus filled Atalanta's heart with love for her husband.

Wanted: Teenagers to work part-time at local amusement park. June 15-September 15. For information, write to: Mr. Steele, Riverview Amusements, 17 Ferry Road, Berryton, IL 12345.

Sometimes you may see a job ad like the one to the left. To reply to this ad, you would write a **business letter**. A business letter is a formal letter. It is written to an individual or organization for a practical purpose. The parts of a business letter are explained below. Look at the business letter Lennox sent to Mr. Steele.

Heading: The date and your full address.

Inside Address: The name and address of the person who will get the letter.

Greeting: A formal greeting, like Dear Mr. (Name), followed by a colon (:).

Body: A clear and brief statement of your reason for writing.

Closing and Signature: Use a formal closing, such as *Sincerely*. Use a comma after the closing. Sign your name. Then print it below your signature.

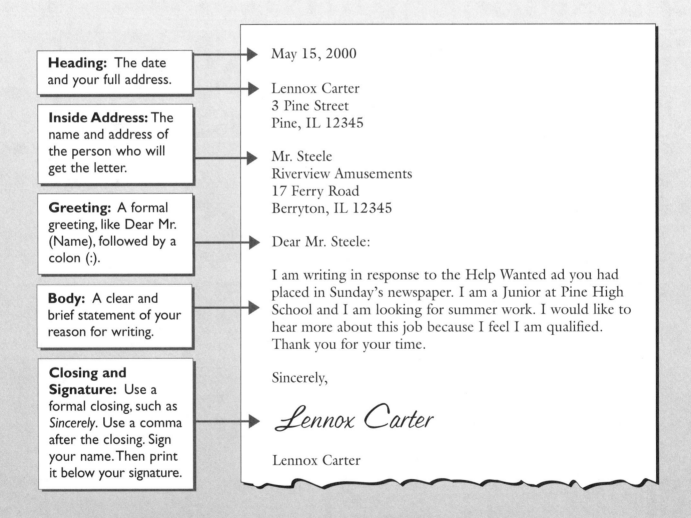

May 15, 2000

Lennox Carter
3 Pine Street
Pine, IL 12345

Mr. Steele
Riverview Amusements
17 Ferry Road
Berryton, IL 12345

Dear Mr. Steele:

I am writing in response to the Help Wanted ad you had placed in Sunday's newspaper. I am a Junior at Pine High School and I am looking for summer work. I would like to hear more about this job because I feel I am qualified. Thank you for your time.

Sincerely,

Lennox Carter

Lennox Carter

YOUR TURN

Ask your teacher to provide you with a blank business letter form. Pick a job you might be interested in and fill out the business letter form.

Chapter Nine

R E V I E W

You have learned a lot already! Look at the checklist and check off what you have learned.

To better understand what I read in English, I:

- ☐ use the dictionary to look up the meanings of new words. (Lesson 1)

- ☐ use the thesaurus to find the right synonyms for words. (Lesson 1)

- ☐ preview a book or story before I read. (Lesson 2)

- ☐ make predictions about what might happen in the story or book. (Lesson 2)

- ☐ ask a question that sets a purpose for reading the story. (Lesson 2)

- ☐ check and update my predictions as I read. (Lesson 2)

- ☐ try to answer the questions I have asked about a story. (Lesson 2)

- ☐ use a story map to keep track of the parts of a story. (Lesson 3)

- ☐ list the story setting, characters, and problem as part of my story map. (Lesson 3)

- ☐ list the main events of the plot in my story map. (Lesson 3)

- ☐ describe the solution to the problem on the story map. (Lesson 3)

- ☐ write the theme of the story on the story map. (Lesson 3)

CHAPTER NINE PRACTICE

Answer the following questions about what you have learned in this chapter.

1. Use this dictionary entry to answer the questions.

> **ice berg** \'is bərg\ *n.* [Norwegian *isberg,* ice mountain] 1. a large floating mass of ice that has broken off a glacier 2. a person who shows no feelings 3. iceberg lettuce.

   a. What is the entry word?

   _____

   b. What part of speech is the entry word?

   _____

   c. From what language did the word come into English?

   _____

   d. How many meanings are given for the word?

   _____

   e. Which syllable of the entry word is said louder?

   _____

2. Circle the most precise word in each group.

   a. politician   senator   lawmaker

   b. glistening   bright   shiny

   c. gulp   drink   swallow

   d. pleasant   nice   warmhearted

   e. trip   cruise   journey

   f. car   vehicle   limo

3. Which is *not* part of previewing a story?

   a. thinking about the title

   b. looking at the illustrations

   c. reading the story word for word

   d. skimming through the text

4. Write *true* or *false* for each statement about active reading.

   a. —————— Predicting is guessing what will happen in a story.

   b. —————— You should never change your predictions as you read.

   c. —————— Setting a purpose for reading helps you focus on a story.

   d. —————— Asking a question is a way to set a purpose for reading a story.

   e. —————— As a story answers your questions, you should ask more.

5. Draw a line from each part of a story map to what it tells.

   a. characters   a difficulty that characters face

   b. setting   the events that happen in a story

   c. problem   the people in the story

   d. plot   how the characters solve a problem

   e. solution   where and when the story takes place

   f. theme   the main message of the story

chapter nine

LEARNING STYLES CHECK-IN

Check off the ways you learn best. Then use the suggestions to
help you read for language arts class.

Sound-smart learner

- Read aloud sections of a story to yourself or others. Use
  your voice to suggest ideas and feelings.
- Tape-record your predictions and purpose-setting
  questions. Play them back from time to time while reading.

People-smart learner

- Discuss a book or story with a group of friends.
- Show someone what you do to be an active reader.

Self-smart learner

- Make a list of the new words you find in each story. Write
  the definitions.
- Imagine you are the main character in a story. Think about
  why you act the way you do.

Picture-smart learner

- Use illustrations in the story to make predictions and set a
  purpose for reading.
- Sketch the key scenes of a story. You can sketch the
  characters too.

Action-smart learner

- When you read a story, act out the key scenes.
- Imagine how the story or book might be made into a movie.

Word-smart learner

- Write a review or journal entry that sums up your feelings
  for a book.
- Work on your answers to story questions to make them
  thoughtful and complete.

Chapter
TEN

Mathematics

GENNA MASTERS MATH

Last term, Genna went to math class every day. She listened to her math teacher. She watched the teacher work out problems on the board. Genna looked at her math book too. She thought she understood most lessons. Even so, Genna almost didn't pass the course. How could that be?

After talking with her teacher, Genna decided to change her approach to math. She now realizes that math has its own language. It has its own words, like *fraction, decimal,* and *triangle.* It has its own symbols, such as $\div$, $>$, and $=$. To do better in math, Genna has to speak the math language.

Genna also decided that learning math is like building a house. You need a solid basement before you build the upstairs of a house. Now Genna is going back and practicing math facts and basic skills. She also takes notes in math class.

Finally, Genna is thinking math. She tries to see math in everyday situations. For example, she calculated the area of her bedroom. She even figured out her batting average in softball.

What happened? Genna is doing better on her tests this term. More important, she has learned that math can be interesting and fun!

What Do You Think?

▶ What words and signs of the math language are hard for you?

▶ Are there some basic math skills you never really learned?

LESSON 1
How to Use Resources

Look at some resources that will help you in math: a calculator, a multiplication chart, and graphs.

Take a Look

CALCULATOR

A calculator is a great math resource. It does arithmetic for you. Do you know how to use one? Find the keys with the +, −, ×, ÷, and = signs. These signs stand for math operations.

to add, press the $+$ key

to subtract, press the $-$ key

to multiply, press the $\times$ key

to divide, press the $\div$ key

to get the answer, press the $=$ key

Suppose you want to add 740 and 560 on a calculator. Enter 740. Then press the + key for addition. Then enter 560. Finally, press the = key. Your answer should be 1300.

To subtract 560 from 740, first enter 740. Then press the − key for subtraction. Next, enter 560. Finally, press the = key. Your answer should be 180.

Here are a few more examples:

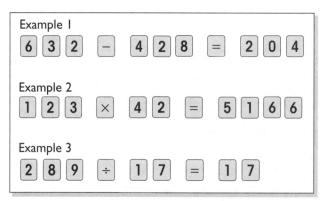

Example 1

6 3 2 − 4 2 8 = 2 0 4

Example 2

1 2 3 × 4 2 = 5 1 6 6

Example 3

2 8 9 ÷ 1 7 = 1 7

GRAPHS

Graphs are another math resource. Graphs use circles, bars, or lines to show information. The title tells what the graph shows. Labels on the graph name the information that is given.

CIRCLE GRAPHS

A circle graph is a circle divided into sections. Each section shows part of the whole, 100%. To read a circle graph, check the title. Read the labels for each section. Then compare the size of the sections. The circle graph on the right shows that most of our mail—62%—is advertising.

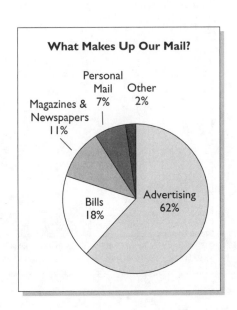

What Makes Up Our Mail?

Personal Mail 7%
Other 2%
Magazines & Newspapers 11%
Bills 18%
Advertising 62%

LINE GRAPHS

A line graph shows change over time. On the left of a line graph is an up-and-down line (vertical axis). It shows the information that is measured. At the bottom of the graph is a side-to-side line (horizontal axis). This line usually measures time. The line graph here, for example, shows that the price of gas was about 26 cents a gallon in 1950 and went up to 31 cents in 1960.

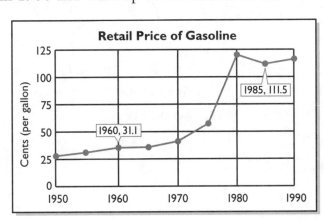

Retail Price of Gasoline

Cents (per gallon)

1985, 111.5

1960, 31.1

BAR GRAPHS

A bar graph usually compares information. One axis shows the items that are measured or compared. The other axis lists numbers. Compare the heights of the bars. These show differences among the items. This bar graph, for example, shows that a load of laundry takes four times more water (40 gallons) than a two-minute shower (10 gallons).

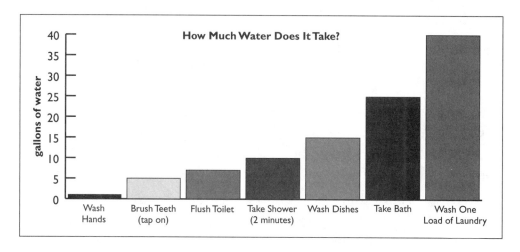

Try It Out

Answer the following questions. Use your calculator to figure out the answers.

1. Use the circle graph on page 139. What percentage of our mail is made up of bills and personal mail? Remember, this question is asking you to add these two figures.

2. Use the line graph on page 139. What was the retail price of gasoline in 1980?

3. Use the bar graph. How much less water does a shower take than a bath? Remember, this question is asking you to find the difference between these two numbers.

On Your Own

Use your calculator and the graphs to answer the questions on the next page, using a separate sheet of paper.

1. How much of our mail is newspapers and magazines? What forms 18% of our mail?

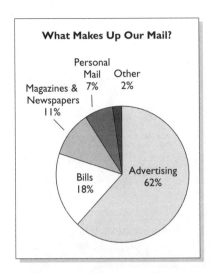

2. How much did gas cost in 1980? Did it go up or down between 1980 and 1990? _____

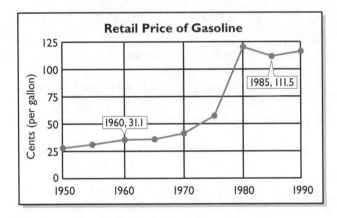

3. How much water does it take to wash the dishes? What activity uses about 5 gallons of water? _____

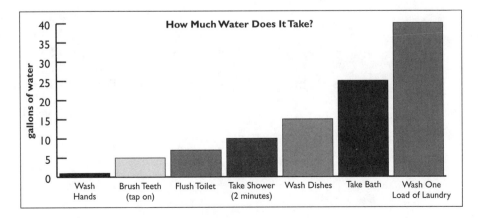

LESSON 2
Problem Solving

You will often have to solve story problems in math. (You might call them word problems.) Look at some skills to solve these problems.

Take a Look

First, remember that all story problems have two main parts. One part gives the information you need. It usually comes first.

If Duane packs his lunch each day, he spends about $10.50 for a five-day week. If he buys lunch from the lunch wagon at work, he spends about $3.50 a day. How much does Duane save each week by packing lunch?

The second part of a story problem asks a question. It usually comes last.

Each story problem is different. These steps will help you solve most story problems.

- Read the problem over a few times. Find the information that is given. Find the question that is asked.

- Write down the information that you will need. It helps to use a chart or drawing.

- Make the change from words to math. That means you have to think in terms of numbers (1, 2, 3) and operations (+, −, ×, ÷).

- Write a math statement that you can use to solve the problem.

- Decide whether you will need one or more operations. Write the additional math statements you will need.

- Solve the problem.

Let's see how Reynaldo solves the story problem.

> If Duane packs his lunch each day, he spends about $10.50 for a five-day week. If he buys lunch from the lunch wagon at work, he spends about $3.50 a day. How much does Duane save each week by packing lunch?

The problem tells Reynaldo that bringing lunch for a week costs less than buying it. He must find out how much less. To begin, he lists information from the problem in a small chart.

	1 day	5 days
brings lunch	?	$10.50
buys lunch	$3.50	?

Reynaldo rereads the problem. He looks again at the chart. He sees that he needs to know how much Duane spends when he buys lunch for five days. To find out, Reynaldo thinks about what math operation to use. Since there are 5 days in a week, he could add $3.50 five times. Or he could multiply $3.50 by 5. Reynaldo decides to multiply. He writes this math statement:

$3.50 × 5 = $17.50

Then he adds this new information to his chart:

	1 day	5 days
brings lunch	?	$10.50
buys lunch	$3.50	$17.50

Again, Reynaldo looks back at the problem. It asks how much Duane saves by bringing lunch for a week. Reynaldo sees that the problem has a second step. A second operation is needed.

To find the savings, Reynaldo decides to subtract the cost of bringing lunch from the cost of buying it. He writes the second math statement:

$$\$17.50 - \$10.50 = \$7.00$$

So, Duane saves $7.00 a week by packing his lunch.

Try It Out

Read this story problem.

> To get back and forth to work, Marla spends $3 a day on bus fare. She pays $4 for lunch each day. In all, how much does she spend on bus fare and lunch for a five-day week?

Show the information from the problem in chart form.

	Day	Week
Bus Fare	_____	_____
Lunch	_____	_____

Look back at the problem. This problem, too, has several parts. Decide what you need to find out first. What math operation will help you find it? In the space below, write two math statements that will give you information you need.

_____

_____

Add this new information to the chart above.

Again, look back at the problem. The problem asks you how much Marla spends in all. What math operation will help you find it?

Write the math statement that will let you find out. This is the solution to the problem.

_____

_____

Check your solution with a friend. You should have found that Marla spends $35 a week on bus fare and lunch.

Reading story problems carefully will help you make the change from words to math operations. Usually there are clue words in a story problem. The clue words suggest what math operation to use.

Here are some clue words and phrases from story problems. Each is listed under the math operation it can suggest.

Addition	Subtraction	Multiplication	Division
sum of	decreased by	times	how much per
how many	less than	percent of	divided
plus	taken away	product of	quotient
total	difference	each	into how many
more	how many are left	equal	in equal amounts
in all	reduced	total	how many times
altogether	how much is saved	in all	each

On Your Own

Read this story problem. Circle the information you need to solve the problem. Underline the question you need to answer. Then answer the question on a separate sheet of paper.

> Don drives his car to work five days a week. He spends about $24 a week on gas. Parking costs $4.50 a day. He takes home $210 a week. How much is left after he pays his driving costs?

LESSON 3
Note Taking in Mathematics

To do well in math class, you will need to take notes. Often, your math teacher will work out problems on the board. Copy every step of each problem. Even if you understand the problem, it is still a good idea to copy the steps.

Sometimes, you might not be able to follow every step. Take notes anyway. Put question marks next to the confusing steps. After class, go over them with your teacher or a study buddy.

Take A Look

Remember, your notes should always include:

- facts or ideas that the teacher repeats several times

- facts or ideas that are circled or underlined on the board

- information that the teacher says will be on a test

One goal of note taking is to get the most down while writing the least. A system of math abbreviations will help.

THREE-COLUMN MATH NOTES

A three-column chart is a good way to organize math notes. Divide a notebook page into three columns. The first column has the heading *Key Idea*. The key idea names the main point or topic of a lesson. You can also write the text page numbers that discuss a key idea. That will make studying easier.

The heading for the second column is *Discussion of Rules*. This is the place to write the important rules that apply. Use phrases and abbreviations to record the rules. If you are unsure of something, you might skip one or two lines in your notes. Later you can fill it in.

The third column is *Examples*. Use this column to write examples that show the rules. Again, if you are unsure about a step, put a question mark next to it.

Here are the three-column notes that one student took for a lesson on subtracting fractions.

Key Idea	Discussion of Rules	Examples
Subtracting fractions	Need a least common denominator	$\dfrac{1}{2} - \dfrac{1}{3}$
(text pp. 44-45)	LCD is 6	
	Multiply each fraction by one	$\dfrac{1}{2} \times \dfrac{3}{3} - \dfrac{1}{3} \times \dfrac{2}{2}$
	Subtract	$\dfrac{3}{6} - \dfrac{2}{6}$
	Simplify if necessary	$\dfrac{1}{6}$

MATH SYMBOLS AND ABBREVIATIONS

Here are some handy symbols and abbreviations to use in your math notes:

Symbol	Meaning
e.g.	for example
∴	therefore
∟	angle
△	triangle
□	square
○	circle
<	less than
>	greater than
=	equal to
→	implies
LCD	least common denominator
asc law	associative law

Try It Out

Fill in the three-column chart on the next page. The key idea here is *adding fractions*. Adding fractions is similar to subtracting fractions. You need a least common denominator. You also need to multiply each fraction by one. After adding, you must simplify the fractions if necessary.

In the example column, work the problem $\frac{1}{4} + \frac{1}{3}$. As you probably know, the least common denominator for this problem is 12. Look back at the chart on page 147 if you need help filling in the columns.

Key Idea	Discussion of Rules	Examples
Adding Fractions		

Note taking does not end when the bell rings. It is often necessary to rework your notes. Most forgetting occurs right after class. So rework your notes as soon as possible—such as in study hall or at home.

These steps will help you rework your math notes:

- Rewrite any notes you cannot read or do not understand. Look for any question marks you made. Rewriting is a way to make sure you understand the key ideas.

- Fill in the gaps. You may not have had time in class to note everything. Find what you missed. Fill in any steps or ideas that you left out. If you skipped lines while taking notes, the gaps are easy to find.

- Review your notes. Once you have reworked your notes, review them. Sum up the key ideas and how to use them.

- Review notes from the past few lessons. Think about how they connect with what you have just learned. New key ideas usually build on what you have learned over the past few weeks.

On Your Own

Use this three-column chart to take notes in your next math class. There may be more than one key idea. As you take notes, leave space for ideas and steps you will want to rework later.

After class, rework your notes.

Key Idea	Discussion of Rules	Examples

A checking account makes handling money easier than just using cash. You have to keep careful track of your account balance though. Your balance is how much money is in the account.

DEPOSIT SLIP

Each time you put money in your checking account, you fill out a deposit slip. This piece of paper shows how much money you are putting in the bank. Cash goes on one line of the deposit slip. The amounts of any checks go on separate lines.

CHECK

When writing checks, always use a pen. Be sure to write clearly. You will have to write the amount in words and numbers. Make sure the two amounts are the same.

YOUR TURN

Now fill in the check below. Make it payable to the L&M Grocery Store. The amount is $35.45. Use today's date.

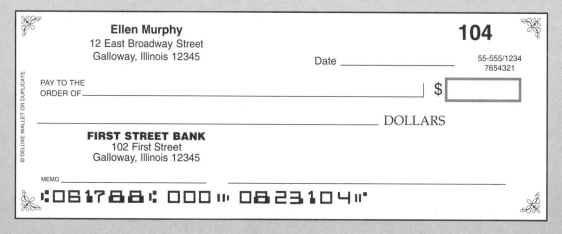

Chapter Ten

R E V I E W

You have learned a lot already! Look at the checklist and check off what you have learned.

To do better in math, I:

- [ ] know how to use a calculator. (Lesson 1)

- [ ] have mastered basic multiplication and division facts. (Lesson 1)

- [ ] know how to use graphs. (Lesson 1)

- [ ] look for the basic information in story problems. (Lesson 2)

- [ ] find the questions being asked in story problems. (Lesson 2)

- [ ] use charts and sketches to help me solve story problems. (Lesson 2)

- [ ] look for clue words that suggest the math operation to use in a problem. (Lesson 2)

- [ ] use math symbols and abbreviations in my notes. (Lesson 3)

- [ ] use a three-column chart to organize math notes. (Lesson 3)

- [ ] use question marks in my notes to mark ideas I do not understand. (Lesson 3)

- [ ] skip lines in my notes for ideas I want to develop further on my own. (Lesson 3)

- [ ] rework and review my notes after class. (Lesson 3)

Answer the following items about what you have learned in this chapter.

1. Which keys on the calculator would you press

    a. to add 31 and 187? _____

    b. to multiply 35 by 17? _____

    c. to subtract 128 from 987? _____

    d. to divide 144 by 11? _____

2. Use this bar graph to answer the following questions.

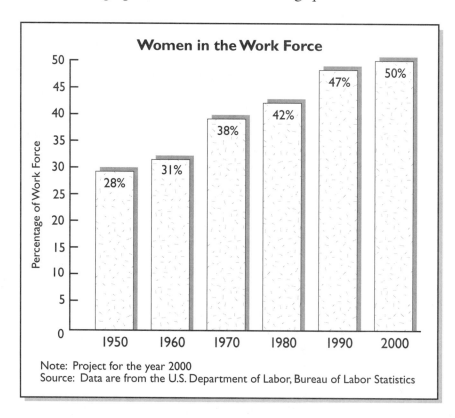

a. In 1950, what percentage of the work force was made up of

women? _____

b. In which year did women make up 47% of the work force?

_____

3. Use the circle graph below to answer the following questions.

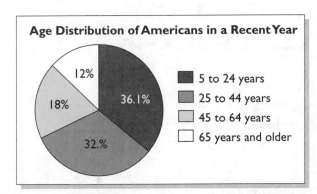

Age Distribution of Americans in a Recent Year

- 5 to 24 years
- 25 to 44 years
- 45 to 64 years
- 65 years and older

12%
18%
36.1%
32.%

a. What percentage of Americans is between 45 and 64 years old? _____

b. What age group has the largest percentage of Americans?

_____

4. Follow these steps to solve the story problem below.

- Read the story problem.

- List the information you need in a chart.

- Choose a math operation to find information you need.

- Write and solve a math statement.

- Add the new information to the chart.

- Choose and complete a second operation, if necessary.

Jack's take-home pay is $215 a week. Parking at the job costs $14 a week. He also spends $3.50 a day on lunch. After paying for parking and lunch, how much of Jack's take-home pay is left?

LEARNING STYLES CHECK-IN

Check off the ways you learn best. Then use the suggestions to help you develop math skills and understand math concepts.

Sound-smart learner

- Arrange to have a seat in class where you can clearly hear and see the teacher.

People-smart learner

- Hold a group math study session. Each member of the group should prepare a few story problems for the group. Do the problems alone. Then check and discuss the problems as a group.

Self-smart learner

- As you study, make a list of questions to help you understand material better. If you are shy about asking questions, write them down and read them to your teacher.

Picture-smart learner

- Draw diagrams and sketches to sum up the information in math problems.

Action-smart learner

- Work problems on the classroom chalkboard whenever possible.
- Use cut-outs and other objects for hands-on math practice.

Word-smart learner

- Write your own story problems for the key ideas you are studying. To make them interesting, use real-life situations.

Number-smart learner

- Take each math concept you learn a step further. Find a new way to apply the skill. Share what you know with a friend.

Chapter

ELEVEN

Social Science

CARMEN CONQUERS

Carmen has to read a chapter in her social science text. The topic is the United States Civil War. Before she reads, Carmen thinks about the topic. She tries to recall what she already knows. Then the new information will make more sense.

As she reads, Carmen looks at the graphics. Besides photographs, she finds timelines, tables, and maps. Each graphic has a lot of information. Studying them gives her a good feel for the subject.

Carmen also takes notes. Taking notes helps her learn. The facts and ideas from her text may be on a test. So the notes will be handy when she has to study.

What happened? Carmen has taken the time to preview her reading. She also remembered to study the graphics in her textbook. Finally, she took notes from her textbook.

In this chapter, we will look at the methods Carmen used. These methods are not hard. You probably use some of them already. With these study methods, you can do much better in social science.

What Do You Think?

▶ What problems have you had in social science?

▶ What does Carmen do to be an active reader?

LESSON 1
How to Use Resources

There are three important resources in social science: timelines, tables, and maps.

Take a Look

READING TIMELINES

A timeline shows the order of events. A timeline is divided into equal periods, usually years. Look to the left for the earliest event. Then read from left to right. A timeline lists when events happened. It also shows how much time passed between events.

The events on a timeline usually tell about one topic. The title of a timeline tells what the topic is.

Here is a timeline from Carmen's social science book. It covers the years 1860–1863. Its title is *The Civil War Begins*. This timeline lists major events of the war.

The first event on the timeline is the election of President Lincoln in November of 1860. In July of 1861, the first major battle of the war, Bull Run, was fought.

The Civil War Begins

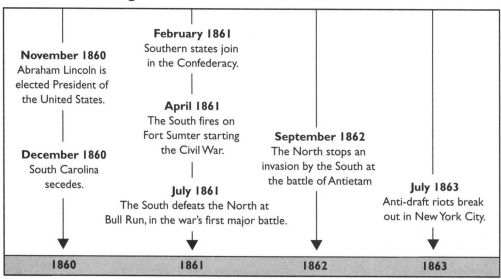

November 1860
Abraham Lincoln is elected President of the United States.

December 1860
South Carolina secedes.

February 1861
Southern states join in the Confederacy.

April 1861
The South fires on Fort Sumter starting the Civil War.

July 1861
The South defeats the North at Bull Run, in the war's first major battle.

September 1862
The North stops an invasion by the South at the battle of Antietam

July 1863
Anti-draft riots break out in New York City.

1860   1861   1862   1863

READING TABLES

Tables show a lot of facts. The facts can be numbers or words. To read a table, first look at the title. It tells you what to expect. The title of the table below is *Major Battles of the Civil War*.

Next look at the columns and rows in the table. The columns go up and down. The rows go across. Usually, the columns have headings. The heading of the first column is *Battle*. The headings of the other columns are *State*, *Date*, and *Casualties: North and South*.

How many Northern soldiers were casualties—killed or wounded— at the battle of Chancellorsville? To find out, go down the *Battle* column to *Chancellorsville*. Then go across the row to the *North Casualties* column. The table says that 11,000 Northerners were casualties in that battle.

Major Battles of the Civil War

Battle	State	Date	Casualties North	South
Antietam	Maryland	Sept. 1862	12,500	10,750
Bull Run	Virginia	Aug. 1862	10,000	9,000
Chancellorsville	Virginia	May 1863	11,000	10,000
Chicamauga	Georgia	Sept. 1863	11,500	17,000
Fredericksburg	Virginia	Dec. 1862	12,000	5,000
Gettysburg	Pennsylvania	July 1863	17,500	22,500
Murfreesboro	Tennessee	Jan. 1863	9,000	9,000
Shiloh	Tennessee	Apr. 1862	13,000	10,500
Vicksburg	Mississippi	May 1863	9,000	10,000

READING MAPS

A map is a drawing of a place or region. Maps are an important resource in social science. Most maps have these parts:

Title: The title tells what information is on the map.

Key: The key shows what the colors and symbols stand for.

Scale: The scale shows the real distance between places.

Compass: The compass shows north, south, east, and west.

Look at the map below. Its title is *The Civil War, 1861–1862*.

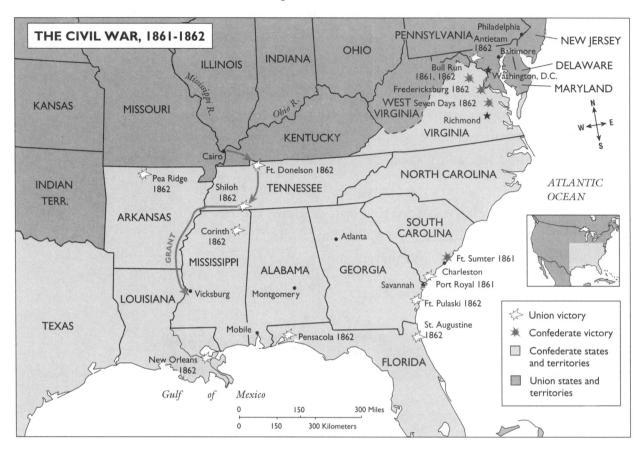

Find the key on the map. The boxes show shades of blue. For example, the lightest blue means "Confederate states and territories." The states in the South are the lightest blue. They were in the Confederacy.

The key also uses a white star to show a Union victory. It uses a blue star to show a Confederate victory.

Try It Out

Use the timeline on page 156 to answer these questions.

1. What happened in April 1861?

_____

_____

2. In what year and month did the South secede from the Union?

_____

Use the table on page 157 to answer these questions.

3. When was the Battle of Fredericksburg fought? _____

4. What were the Southern casualties at Gettysburg? _____

Use the map on page 158 to answer these questions.

5. Which battle took place farthest west? _____

6. Who won the Battle of Shiloh? _____

On Your Own

Study the timeline, the table, and the map on pages 156–158.
Then answer the following questions.

1. In what year and month did the Battle of Bull Run take place?

   _____

   _____

2. How many casualties did the North suffer in the Battle
   of Bull Run?

   _____

   _____

3. Who won the Battle of Bull Run?

   _____

   _____

4. What event took place in September 1862?

   _____

   _____

5. In what year did the Battle of New Orleans take place?

   _____

6. What were the total number of casualties in the Battle of
   Gettysburg?

   _____

LESSON 2

Active Reading

Key Term

K-W-L chart chart that lists what you know about a topic, what you want to know, and what you learned

Active players make the best athletes. These athletes use everything they know about the game. They work to learn new skills. They also learn each time they play.

Take a Look

Active readers make good students. Active readers use what they know. They think about what they want to learn. They also keep track of what they do learn.

Here are three steps to become a more active reader:

1. Before you read, recall what you already know about a topic.

2. Ask questions about what you want to learn.

3. As you read, write down what you learn.

Carmen is about to read part of her social science text. From the heading, she knows it is about African Americans in the Civil War. To be an active reader, Carmen decides to use a **K-W-L chart**. A K-W-L chart lists what you know, what you want to know, and what you learned. In the first column of the chart, she lists what she knows about the topic. In the second column, she asks a few questions. She hopes the section will answer these questions. After she finishes reading, Carmen will list what she learned in the third column.

Read this section from Carmen's text on the next page. Then look at how she completes the K-W-L chart.

African Americans in the Civil War

One group of people especially helped the Union side. They were African Americans. More than 200,000 African Americans served in the Union army and navy. Many had escaped from slavery in the South to fight for freedom.

African Americans who fought for the Union faced danger in battle. They also faced hardship behind their own lines. They were paid less than whites. Often, they were given the hardest jobs.

The 54th Massachusetts Volunteer Infantry was an African American regiment in the Union army. On July 10, 1863, the 54th attacked a fort outside Charleston, South Carolina. Confederate bullets and cannon shells rained down on the soldiers. Almost half of the soldiers in the 54th were killed.

African Americans fought bravely under fire. The U.S. Secretary of War praised them to President Lincoln. He said they "have proved themselves the bravest of the brave." Twenty African Americans won the Congressional Medal of Honor for bravery. Almost 40,000 died in the war.

K	W	L
WHAT I KNOW	WHAT I WANT TO KNOW	WHAT I LEARNED
Many slaves ran away to join the Union Army.	How many African Americans fought in the war?	Over 200,00 served in the Union Army and Navy.
African Americans were paid less than white soldiers.	What were some African American regiments?	The 54th Massachusetts Volunteer Infantry

Try It Out

The next section is about the military goals of the North and the South in the Civil War. Use the K-W-L chart to read actively. Carmen read the following in her textbook. Read the selection and complete the K-W-L chart that Carmen began.

The Goals of the North and the South

The North had a three-part plan. First, it wanted to take control of the Mississippi River. That way, the South would be split in two. Second, the North wanted to capture Richmond, Virginia. That was the Confederate capital. Third, the Union navy wanted to blockade the South. Its ships tried to shut off Southern ports. If the ports were closed, the South could not sell cotton. It could not buy supplies in Europe either.

The South tried to hold off attacks from the North. The South hoped Northerners would grow tired of war. They might accept the Confederacy. People in the South also hoped France and England would help them. Those countries needed Southern cotton for their factories. To get their help, though, the Confederacy had to win battles.

K	W	L
WHAT I **K**NOW	WHAT I **W**ANT TO KNOW	WHAT I **L**EARNED
The North and South had different goals.		
	How did the South think they could win the Civil War?	The South hoped France and England would help them.

On Your Own

The last part of this social science chapter is given below. It is about the early fighting in the Civil War.

Early Fighting in the East

In the early years of the war, the Union army in the East faced hard times. The Union soldiers were as brave as the Confederates. They had more supplies too. But they lacked good generals.

The South had found a great general. Robert E. Lee of Virginia took charge of Confederate troops in the East in 1862. He was helped by many able officers.

The North wanted to capture Richmond, Virginia. Again and again, it moved its troops south. Each time, Robert E. Lee found a way to defeat them.

Lee had so much success that he decided to invade the North. In September 1862, the two armies clashed at Antietam (an-TEE-tum) Creek in Maryland. It was the bloodiest day of the war. More than 26,000 men were lost. The Union stopped Lee's invasion. But it did not chase the retreating Southerners. Lee's army survived to fight again.

On a separate sheet of paper, make a K-W-L chart. Fill in the first two columns before you read. Then read the passage and fill in the third column.

K	W	L
WHAT I KNOW	WHAT I WANT TO KNOW	WHAT I LEARNED

LESSON 3

Note Taking in Social Science

Each paragraph in a social science text usually has one main idea. It has several important details too. Taking notes is the best way to learn this information.

In this lesson, you will read another social science passage about the Civil War. For each paragraph, you'll take notes. Your notes will show the main idea and important details. You will get a chance to take notes in different ways. You will use a pyramid, an outline, and a word web. You learned these methods of note taking in Chapter 6.

Take a Look

Remember . . .

- To find the main idea of a paragraph, ask, "What does the author most want me to learn?"
- To find important details, ask, "Which information best supports or shows the main idea?"
- Write your notes in your own words.
- Use a note-taking style that you like.

 For more about note pyramids, see page 76.

Read the two paragraphs on the top of page 165 and Keisha's notes. Notice how Keisha used a note pyramid to record her notes.

President Lincoln decided to **emancipate**, or free, the slaves. He hoped the free slaves would run away. With fewer slaves, the South would get less work done. Lincoln also knew that the South wanted help from England and France. Those countries had outlawed slavery long ago. They would be less likely to help the South in a war against slavery. Finally, Lincoln wanted to give Northerners a new reason for fighting. He wanted them to fight for justice for African Americans.

On January 1, 1863, President Lincoln issued the Emancipation Proclamation. It freed slaves in areas fighting against the United States. It did not free slaves in the border states. African Americans welcomed the order. It was a big step toward the end of slavery.

Main Ideas: President Lincoln emancipated slaves to weaken the South.

The Emancipation Proclamation was a major step toward ending slavery

Details: Emancipated slaves would be more likely to run away. France and England would be less likely to help the South in a war against slavery. The Emancipation did not free all slaves, only those in the Confederacy. The Emancipation Proclamation was on January 1, 1863.

Point President Lincoln freed the slaves in 1863.

For more about note outlines, see page 80.

Try It Out

Continue reading the passage. Use the following outline below to take notes. Remember: The main ideas go next to the Roman numerals. The important details go next to the capital letters.

The Union had its greatest success in the West. The navy, under Latino commander, David Farragut, played a big role. In 1862, Farragut's ships took New Orleans. Then they sailed up the Mississippi River. This brought much of the river under Union control.

Meanwhile, the Union Army under General Ulysses S. Grant fought its way south from Tennessee. By late 1862, Grant's troops had reached Mississippi. They were stopped at Vicksburg. Cannons in the city gave the Confederates control of the river there.

Grant wanted to take Vicksburg. For months, he shelled the city. Union soldiers cut off food. Finally, in July 1863, Vicksburg surrendered. The Union controlled the Mississippi River. The South had been cut in two.

I. _The Union had its greatest success in the West._

    A. _____

    B. _____

II. _____

    A. _In late 1862, Grant's troops reached Mississippi._

    B. _____

III. _____

    A. _____

    B. _In July 1863, Vicksburg surrendered._

On Your Own

Here are the last paragraphs of the passage on the Civil War. As you read, show your notes on a web. List the main idea of each paragraph. List the details that tell about it.

For more about note webs, see page 78.

The South continued to win in the East. So in June of 1863, General Lee decided to invade the North. He hoped that if the South won a victory there, the North would quit. Lee's army reached Pennsylvania before the fighting began. The two armies clashed at Gettysburg on July 1, 1863. Three bitter days of fighting followed.

On the first day, the Confederates pushed Union troops back. On the next two days, though, the Union turned back the attacks. On July 3, Lee sent 13,000 troops to charge Union lines. Almost half of Lee's soldiers were killed. The rest were driven back. The next day, Lee's army began to retreat south.

Lee had lost the Battle of Gettysburg. His defeat ended the South's hope of winning the war. Four months later, President Lincoln came to Gettysburg. There he gave the Gettysburg Address. The speech praised the soldiers who had died. Lincoln reminded the nation that the war meant freedom for all.

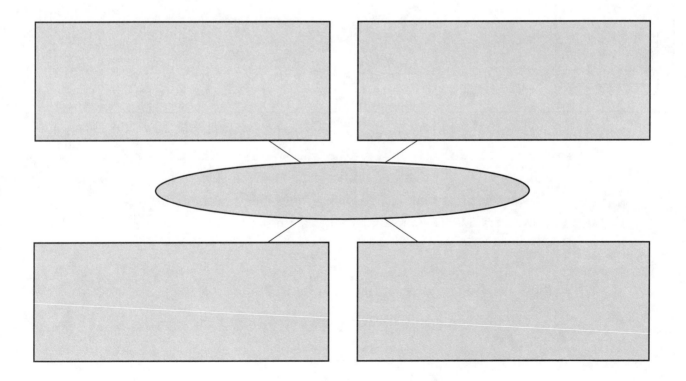

You use a map when you want directions from one place to another. When you want to figure out the distance between two places you use a scale of miles. You can also use the compass to find out what direction you are driving in.

This is a map of Southern California. To figure out the distance between Garden Grove and La Mirada, look at the scale of miles. An inch represents 5 miles. The distance between Garden Grove and La Mirada measures 1 inch. The total distance in miles between Garden Grove and La Mirada is 5 miles.

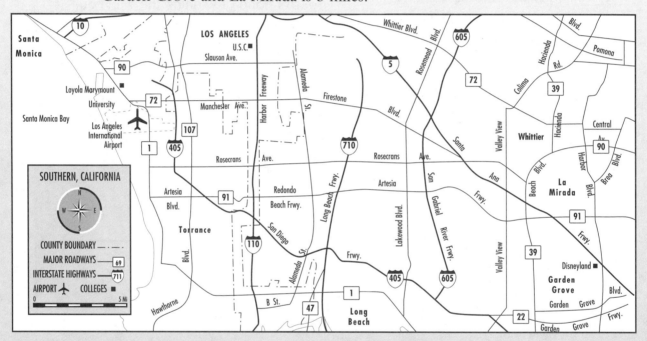

Lucy wants to travel from her home in Long Beach to Garden Grove. She wants to know how far she will have to drive. Using a ruler, she measures the distance on the map. It is 3 inches. Then she looks at the scale. One inch equals 5 miles. She multiplies 5 by 3 and discovers that Torrance is 15 miles from her house.

YOUR TURN

Use the scale of miles to answer this question.

What is the shortest distance between Interstate 710 and Disneyland?

Chapter Eleven

REVIEW

You have learned a lot already! Look at the checklist and check off what you have learned.

To better understand what I read in social science, I:

☐ read the titles of timelines, tables, and maps. (Lesson 1)

☐ note how many years each part of a timeline stands for. (Lesson 1)

☐ read the title and column headings to find out what's in a table. (Lesson 1)

☐ read across the rows and down the columns to find facts in a table. (Lesson 1)

☐ read the key of a map to find out what the colors symbols stand for. (Lesson 1)

☐ use the map compass to find directions and the map scale to find distances. (Lesson 1)

☐ list what I know about a social science topic before I read. (Lesson 2)

☐ ask myself what I want to know about a topic. (Lesson 2)

☐ sum up what I have learned after reading a passage. (Lesson 2)

☐ look for the main ideas and details in each paragraph of a passage. (Lesson 3)

☐ use a note pyramid, an outline, or a word web to take notes. (Lesson 3)

Answer the following items about what you have learned in this chapter.

1. Use the timeline to answer the questions.

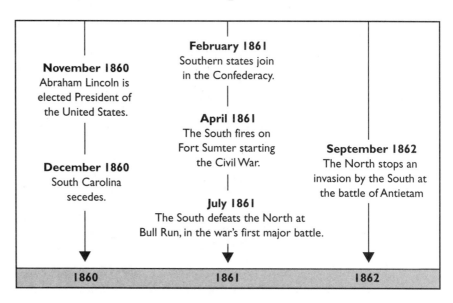

a. Timelines are divided into equal periods of time. How many years are in each period of this timeline? _____

b. When did the Civil War start? _____

2. The passage below tells about the hard life that early settlers faced on the Plains. On a separate sheet of paper, create a K-W-L chart. Fill in the first two columns first. Then read the passage. Finally, fill in the last column.

A Hard Life

New settlers faced a harsh world on the Plains. The hot sun baked them in summer. In winter, storms pushed snow over rooftops. The grass on the Plains had thick roots. This was called **sod**. Sod made planting crops hard. Often, rainfall was scarce. There were few trees for fences.

> Still, the settlers stayed on. They learned to use steel plows. These plows cut through the thick sod. They drilled deep wells for water. A new product, barbed wire, was invented in 1874. Wire fences kept animals out of the crops.

3. Take notes on the same passage. On a separate sheet of paper use a note pyramid to show the main ideas, details, and point.

4. Use the map below to answer the questions.

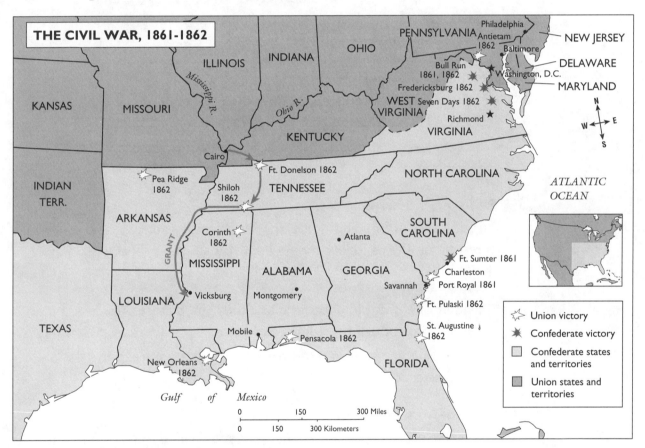

a. Who won the battle of New Orleans? _____

b. In what year was the Battle of Pensacola fought? _____

c. How many battles did Grant win on his way from Cairo to

Vicksburg? _____

chapter eleven

LEARNING STYLES CHECK-IN

Check off the ways you learn best. Then use the suggestions to help you do better in social science.

Sound-smart learner
- Make a K-W-L chart on tape. Record what you know and what you want to learn. After reading, record any answers you found and what you learned.

People-smart learner
- Talk to other students about how they use their social science texts. What do they do to learn and remember?
- Stage a K-W-L show. Show other students how to use this method.

Self-smart learner
- Make a list of do's and don'ts for using social science resources. Try to follow them when you study.

Picture-smart learner
- Find books with old photographs. Study the pictures to learn more about other times and places.
- Draw diagrams and sketches to sum up what you read in social science.

Action-smart learner
- Act out some important events that you read about.

Word-smart learner
- Read over the answers you write to study questions. See if you can write a better answer in fewer words.

Number-smart learner
- Make your own timelines for historic events. Use them to study social science.

Chapter
TWELVE

Science

HAI HELPS HIMSELF

When it comes to science, Hai is an active learner. Before reading a science assignment, Hai scans it. This gives him a good idea of what to expect. He also asks questions to focus his reading.

As he reads, Hai "talks back" to his text. That is, he tries to answer the questions he has asked himself. He also asks new questions that come to mind. Hai pays special attention to the graphics and tables in his book. He knows that these show important facts.

Taking notes is another part of active learning. Sometimes Hai sketches diagrams in his notes. Diagrams are a simple way to sum up ideas from the text.

Hai is also familiar with his text. He uses the glossary at the back of the book. Science words can be hard. Fortunately, the glossary lists all of them and their meanings.

What happened? Hai used many different study techniques. He is an active learner in science. Active learners are involved with their schoolwork. Active readers usually understand what they read. Becoming an active learner will help you in science and in other subjects too.

What Do You Think?

▶ What makes Hai an active learner?

▶ Can you think of things you might do to become a more active learner?

LESSON 1
How to Use Resources

A picture is worth a thousand words. That is why diagrams are an important resource in science. Diagrams show the "big picture." They show many facts and details. Diagrams also show processes. They show how things work.

Take a Look

To read a diagram, first check the title. The title shows what the diagram is about. Next, look for labels. The labels name the parts of the diagram.

Here is a diagram from a science text. The title is *The Parts of a Volcano*. That tells you the diagram probably shows a typical volcano. The labels name things about a volcano you should know.

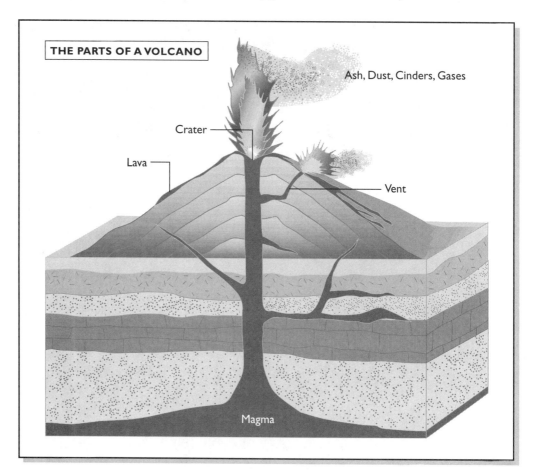

THE PARTS OF A VOLCANO

Ash, Dust, Cinders, Gases

Crater

Lava

Vent

Magma

To begin with, this diagram shows the shape of a volcano. It also shows the layers of the earth beneath the volcano. It lets you see the parts of the volcano too—the magma, the crater, and the vent. What facts can you learn from this diagram?

Here is another science diagram. It looks like a map. Remember to read the title first: *The World's Volcanoes*. That tells you what the diagram shows.

As you look over a diagram, look for a caption. The caption is the text beneath a diagram or picture. This caption tells you most of the volcanoes listed occur where Earth's plates meet. These moving plates lead to new volcanoes being formed.

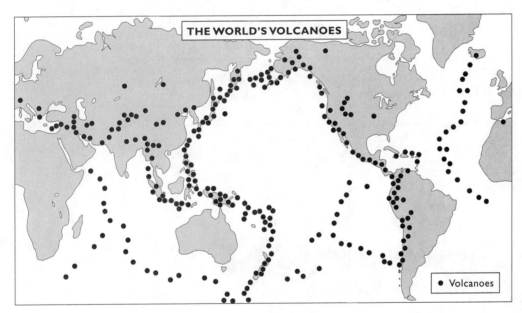

Most of the volcanoes listed occur where the Earth's plates meet. When these plates move, new volcanoes are often formed.

In addition to summing up information, some diagrams have arrows or numbers. Arrows show how one thing leads to another. They might show the direction in which things move. Numbers usually show the steps of a process.

Try It Out

Take a look at these science diagrams. Read the titles, captions, and labels. Think about what the diagrams show.

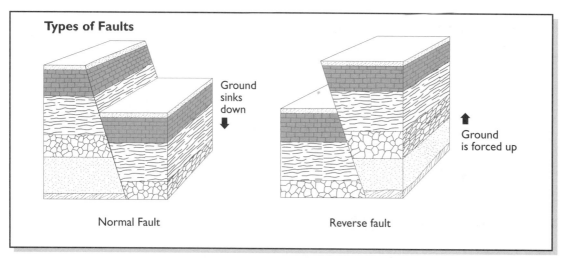

Diagram 1: Types of Faults Magma under the Earth can put pressure on the Earth's crust. A break in Earth's crust is called a **fault**.

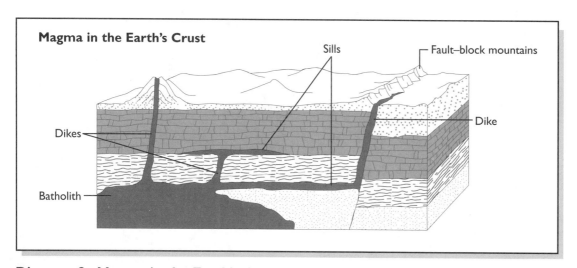

Diagram 2: Magma in the Earth's Crust A mass of hardening magma is a **batholith**. A batholith puts pressure on the rock around it. Cracks form in nearby rocks and fill with magma. If there is movement at the surface along the cracks, mountains may form.

On the following lines, write one fact about each diagram.

Diagram 1: _____

Diagram 2: _____

Sometimes you should draw your own diagrams for science. Diagrams can be part of your notes. A diagram is a quick way to sum up the facts and details that you read. A diagram also shows that you understand how something works.

On Your Own

Read this selection from a science book. It tells how Earth's plates move. How might you use diagrams to show the information?

SCIENCE

1. The plates of Earth's crust move in different ways. Some plates move toward each other. One plate is pushed under another. For example, a plate under an ocean might be pushed under a continental, or land, plate. This can cause mountains to form.

2. Other plates move apart from each other. These plates are often in the oceans. The action of pulling apart forms deep valleys called rifts. When the plates pull apart, magma may break through and form volcanoes.

In the space below or on a separate sheet of paper, sketch a small diagram for each paragraph. Begin with a title. Use labels and arrows to show movement.

1.

2.

LESSON 2

Active Reading

Being active is important in life. It is also important when you read.

Take a Look

 You learned about SQ3R in Chapter 4. See page 52.

SQ3R is a great way to read science. It stands for:

Survey	S
Question	Q
Read	
Record	} 3R
Review.	

Your first step is to survey. That means skim through the text, reading the titles, headings, and key words. Do not read word for word now. The idea is to get a good overview.

The second step is to question. Ask yourself questions about the reading. If you like, turn the chapter headings into questions. Think about what you want to learn about the topic.

Survey and question the passage on page 179 from a science text. Remember, this is not the time to read it word for word. You will do that later.

Look at the following questions Jane asked herself after she surveyed the science text on page 179.

1. How do volcanoes form?

2. What are the parts of a volcano?

3. What are the different types of volcanoes?

A Volcano Is Born

The scene is a cornfield in Mexico. A farmer is working there. It is February 1943. Suddenly, the earth rumbles. Smoke comes out of a hole in the ground. The air smells like rotten eggs.

The next morning the hole is a cone of ash. The cone is 30 feet high. The earth rumbles louder. Rocks start flying out of the hole. By night, the cone is 150 feet high.

The next day things get worse. Melted rock, or lava, comes pouring out. Ten feet of ash and hardened lava cover the field. The explosions get louder. No one can stand nearby. Smoke boils up thousands of feet into the sky.

In two weeks, the cone is 1,500 feet high. Ash and lava cover 15 square miles. The nearby villages are buried. The volcano called Paricutín has been born.

The Parts of a Volcano

Magma is melted rock deep inside the earth. Sometimes, magma breaks through Earth's crust. The opening from which magma flows is called a **vent**. Once on the surface, magma is called lava. Dust, ash, and rock also fly out of the vent. With the lava, they form the **volcanic cone**.

A **volcano** is the vent and the volcanic cone. At the top of the cone is a pit. This pit is called a **crater**. The crater forms when rock and magma are blown out the vent.

Sometimes the top of a volcano explodes. A wide opening is left. This wide opening is a **caldera**. Some calderas fill with water. They form large lakes.

Different Types of Volcanoes

Volcanoes can erupt quietly or explosively. During a quiet eruption, lava flows freely through a vent. Explosive eruptions shoot rocks, lava, and ash high into the air. Different kinds of eruptions form different volcanic cones.

A **shield cone** is formed by quiet eruptions. Lava flows over a large area. It hardens. Many layers of lava build up. They form a cone. The sides of a shield cone are not steep.

A **cinder cone** is made by explosive eruptions. Ash and rock fly out. They pile up to form the cone. Cinder cones have steep sides. They have narrow bases.

A **composite cone** is formed by quiet and explosive eruptions. In a quiet eruption, lava forms a wide base. An explosive eruption adds a layer of ash and rock. Then another quiet eruption adds a layer of lava. In time, a high, wide volcanic cone forms.

The next two steps of SQ3R are **read** and **record**. You already have a good idea what the passage is about. You also have questions that will help you focus your reading. Now it is time to read the pages carefully. Look for the main ideas. Try to answer the questions you have asked.

This is also the time to record, or take notes. Your notes should have all the main ideas and important details.

The last step of SQ3R is **review**. Reviewing sounds easy, but it is very important. For one thing, reviewing helps you learn the information for good! Reviewing also helps you see what you don't fully understand.

There are many ways to review what you have read. Summarizing is one way. A summary is a short version of the text you read. A summary just gives the main ideas and details.

Drawing diagrams is another good way to review. A diagram can help you see information in a new way. Diagrams let you put all the pieces together.

Try It Out

Go back and read the passage about volcanoes. Read it word for word. As you read, use this word web to organize your notes.

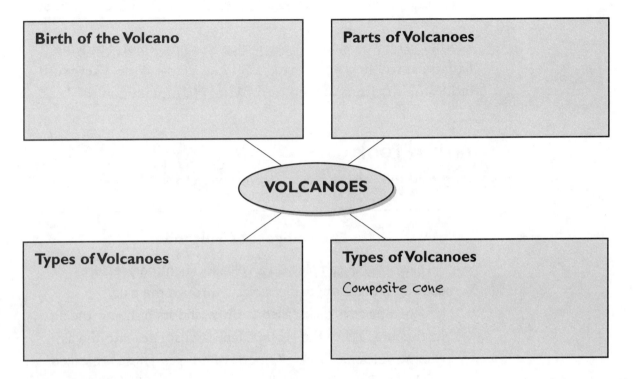

Birth of the Volcano

Parts of Volcanoes

VOLCANOES

Types of Volcanoes

Types of Volcanoes

Composite cone

On Your Own

Review the information in the section titled *Different Types of Volcanoes*. Using the passage and your notes, draw the three types of volcanic cones in the space provided or on a separate sheet of paper.

LESSON 3
Note Taking in Science

Learning key words and ideas in science is important. Studying flash cards will help you. Use 3 x 5 index cards. Write a key word or idea on the front of each card. Write the meaning on the back.

Take A Look

John read this science passage about volcanoes.

The Dangers of Volcanoes

Thick magma can plug up a volcano. Then the pressure builds up. At last, trapped gas blasts through the plug. Hardened magma rock, called **tephra**, shoots high into the air. Most tephra falls to the ground. Tephra dust rises into the air.

Some volcanoes give off floods of hot gas. These are called **proclastic flows**. The deadly gases can be 1,400°F. The gas travels close to the ground at speeds over 100 miles an hour. One such flow from Mount Pelee killed 30,000 people—an entire city—on the island of Martinique in 1902.

Chunks of foamy molten lava can be thrown into the air. These bombs harden in the air into **pumice**. Pumice is a light rock full of holes. The holes are popped gas bubbles. Chunks of pumice weighing tons are found floating in the ocean after a volcano.

A volcanic mudslide is a **lahar**. It is caused by melting snow or heavy rains during an eruption. Water mixes with tephra to form thick mud. In 1985, the volcano Nevado del Ruiz in Colombia triggered a lahar. A 130-foot-high wall of mud killed 22,000 people.

Volcano-safety programs can save lives. Costa Rica, for example, had volcanoes erupt in 1997 and 1998. People there were prepared for the disasters though. So there was no loss of life.

Here are two flash cards that John made. They show key terms from the passage. When John studies, he flips through his flash cards. It is an easy way to review all the key words and concepts.

Front

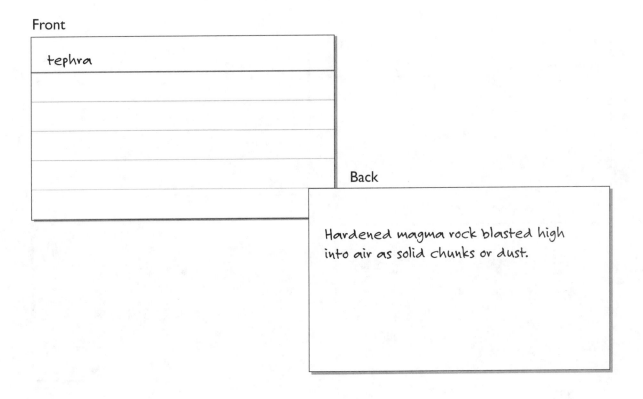

tephra

Back

Hardened magma rock blasted high into air as solid chunks or dust.

Front

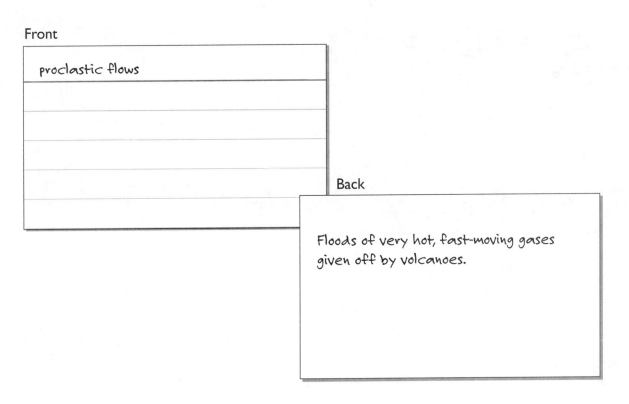

proclastic flows

Back

Floods of very hot, fast-moving gases given off by volcanoes.

Try It Out

Look back at the passage about the dangers of volcanoes. Make flash cards for two key words. Write the meaning on the back. Use the index cards below.

Front

pumice

Back

Front

lahar

Back

On Your Own

Read this passage about lava flows. First find two key words to put on flash cards. Make the flash cards using index cards.

Then, take notes on the passage about lava flows. On a separate sheet of paper, take notes on this passage using a note pyramid. Remember, the main ideas go at the top. The details go next. Then, at the bottom, write the point of the passage.

Lava Flows

Lava is magma that erupts from a volcano. Lava can flow a few inches per day. Or it can race over land at 30 miles per hour. The slope of the mountain determines how fast it goes. So does the lava's temperature.

The heat of lava is deadly. Usually, the flow is too slow to threaten lives. People have time to get out of the way. Homes cannot escape though.

Lava cools and hardens from the outside in. Underneath its hard, shiny-black surface, the lava keeps flowing. The moving lava underneath creates a pattern on the rock above.

Pahoehoe (pah-hoy-hoy) lava has a shiny, wrinkled surface. It looks like coils of rope. The word was borrowed from Hawaiian and means "lava you can walk on." Jagged, rough lava is called **aa** (ah-ah) lava. It means "lava you cannot walk on."

Lava takes a long time to cool. Lava fields in Iceland smoke 15 years after an eruption. Eventually, most lava hardens into a hard black stone called **basalt**. Ground-up basalt is used in cement and road-making. Some lava hardens into a beautiful glass. Native Americans prized this colorful glass called **obsidian**. They used it for arrowheads, knives, and jewelry.

In science we use diagrams to gather information. Sometimes we use science diagrams outside of the classroom.

A nutrition pyramid is a science diagram. It appears on the packaging of different types of food. It is a guide to the different food groups. The pyramid shows how many starches, proteins, fruits and vegetables, and dairy products a person should eat every day.

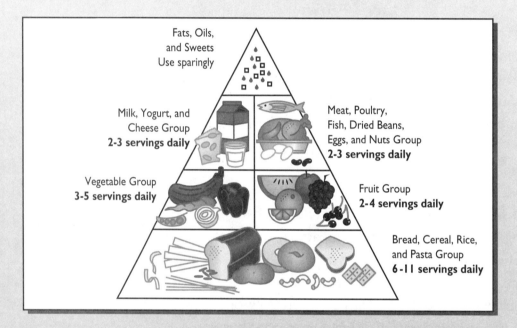

Peter looks at the nutrition pyramid to see how many vegetables he should eat every day. He looks for the section with pictures of different types of vegetables. It shows that he should eat three to five vegetables every day. Peter only ate two vegetables that day. By looking at the chart he knows he needs to eat at least one more vegetable to have a good, balanced diet.

YOUR TURN

Use the pyramid to write a menu for one day: breakfast, lunch, and dinner. Your menu should include the suggested number of servings of each food group on the pyramid.

Breakfast: _____

Lunch: _____

Dinner: _____

Chapter Twelve

REVIEW

You have learned a lot already! Look at the checklist and check off what you have learned. You can add some of your own ideas on the lines following the checklist.

To better understand what I read in science, I:

☐ check the titles and labels on science diagrams. (Lesson 1)

☐ note whether diagrams use arrows to show processes. (Lesson 1)

☐ draw my own diagrams to sum up facts and details. (Lesson 1)

☐ use the SQ3R process when reading my science text. (Lesson 2)

☐ survey and question a reading assignment before reading word for word. (Lesson 2)

☐ read a science passage word for word to answer the questions I have asked. (Lesson 2)

☐ take notes on the passage using a familiar note-taking method. (Lessons 2 and 3)

☐ review each assignment. (Lesson 2)

☐ create flash cards to learn key words and ideas in science. (Lesson 3)

☐ _____

_____

☐ _____

_____

Answer the following items about what you have learned in this chapter.

1. Write two things you can do to become a more active reader in science.

   a. _____

   b. _____

2. Study this diagram of the carbon cycle. Then answer the following question.

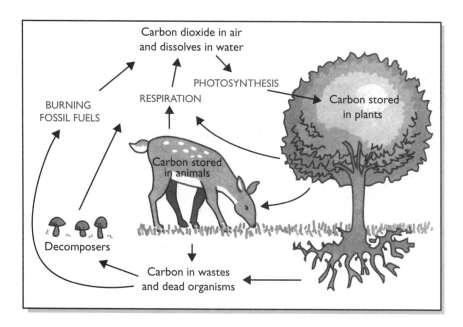

   Name two processes that release carbon dioxide into the air.

   _____

3. Read the following section from a science text. Find the two key words. Then create flash cards for the key words on the next page.

   > Groups of cells that work together doing the same job are called **tissues**. Blood cells work together to make blood tissue. Muscle cells work together to make muscle tissue. Nerve cells work together to make nerve tissue.

Groups of tissues work together to make up an **organ**. Your heart is an organ. Muscle tissue makes your heart pump. Nerve tissues tell it when to pump. Connective tissue holds the parts together. Blood tissue delivers food and oxygen to and from the heart.

Front

Back

Front

Back

4. Answer these questions about the SQ3R method.

   a. When using SQ3R, the first step is to _____, or skim through, the entire reading passage.

   b. The second step is to ask yourself _____ about the passage.

   c. The third step of SQ3R is to _____ the whole passage word for word.

   d. Fourth, _____ or take notes as you read the passage.

   e. Finally, you should _____ the passage and your notes.

LEARNING STYLES CHECK-IN

Check off the ways you learn best. Then use the suggestions to help you do well in science.

Sound-smart learner
- Record the questions you want to focus on when reading. After you read, play back your questions and answer them on tape. Later, use the tapes to study for tests.

People-smart learner
- Stage an SQ3R demonstration. Show other students how to use this method to read a science assignment.

Self-smart learner
- Make your own list of do's and don'ts for studying science. Post them in your study space. Follow them when you study.

Picture-smart learner
- Pay special attention to photos, charts, and diagrams in your science texts.

Action-smart learner
- Take a "hands-on" approach to science. Do experiments and demonstrations that show the main ideas in your science text. Keep careful records of your experiments.

Word-smart learner
- Write some original paragraphs that illustrate the main ideas in your textbooks.

Number-smart learner
- Find ways to use math in science. You might be able to show an idea as an equation. You can also make up some word problems that show the main ideas of a reading assignment.

part **two** ◄ **wrap-up**

In Part 2 you learned about strategies to help you study in language arts, math, social science, and science. Now you can fill in this action plan with all of the things you learned.

The following chart lists the topics of each chapter. Fill in the chart with the most important things you learned. Review this chart the next time you study.

Action Plan

Chapters 9 Through 12
Chapter 9 Language Arts
Chapter 10 Mathematics
Chapter 11 Social Science
Chapter 12 Science

What Do You Think?

Which of the strategies you learned in Part 2 will help you the most?

_____

_____